Aspects of Jewish Culture

in the Middle Ages

Papers of the eighth annual conference of the

Center for Medieval and Early Renaissance Studies

State University of New York at Binghamton

3–5 May 1974

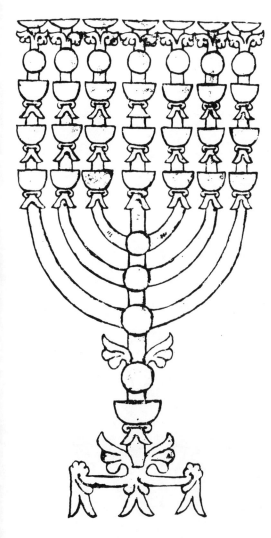

Aspects of Jewish Culture in the Middle Ages

Edited by Paul E. Szarmach

State University of New York Press Albany, 1979

Published by
State University of New York Press
Albany, New York 12246

First Printing 1979

Library of Congress Cataloging in Publication Data

Main entry under title:
Aspects of Jewish culture in the Middle Ages.

   Includes bibliographical references.
   1. Jews—History—70-1789—Historiography—
Congresses. 2. Christianity and antisemitism—
Congresses. 3. Jews in Spain—History—Congresses.
4. Judaism and art—Congresses. 5. Grail—
Congresses. 6. Spain—History—Arab period, 711-
1492—Congresses. I. Szarmach, Paul E.
II. New York (State). State University at Bing-
hamton. Center for Medieval and Early Renaissance
Studies.
DS124.A74   909'.04'924   77-29046
ISBN 0-87395-165-4

CONTENTS

CONTRIBUTORS

YOSEF HAYIM YERUSHALMI
Harvard University

ROSEMARY RADFORD RUETHER
*Garrett-Evangelical Theological Seminary and
Northwestern University*

NORMAN A. STILLMAN
State University of New York at Binghamton

HARRIET GOLDBERG
Villanova University

JOSEPH GUTMANN
Wayne State University

LESLIE A. FIEDLER
State University of New York at Buffalo

INTRODUCTION

Omnia quippe elementa auctorem suum venisse testata sunt. Ut enim de eis quiddam usu humano loquar, Deum hunc coeli esse cognoverunt, quia protinus stellam miserunt. Mare cognovit, quia sub plantis eius se calcabile praebuit. Terra cognovit, quia eo moriente contremuit. Sol cognovit, quia lucis suae radios abscondit. Saxa et parietes cognoverunt, quia tempore mortis eius scissa sunt. Infernus agnovit, quia hos quos tenebat mortuos reddidit. Et tamen hunc, quem Dominum omnia insensibilia elementa senserunt, adhuc infidelium Judaeorum corda Deum esse minime cognoscunt, et, duriora saxis, scindi ad poenitendum nolunt, eumque confiteri abnegant, quem elementa, ut diximus aut signis aut scissionibus Deum clamabant.[1]

Gregory the Great's cosmic indictment of the hard-hearted perversity of the Jews, while no doubt striking for its rhetorical effect, is in many ways a typical text in the history of Jewish-Christian relations. Even when the customarily restrained Aelfric of Eynsham modulates Gregory's stridency by noting in his vernacular adaptation that " . . . [the Jews] were not, however, all equally unbelieving, but of their race there were both prophets and apostles, and many thousands of believing men," the intellectual impulse towards what we now call "majority history," clear and unequivocal in the Latin source, continues on.[2] It is well-known that from the

earliest times the refusal of the Jews to accept Christ
was a perplexity to the Children of the New Law. In
the apocryphal *Visio Pauli*, a weeping Moses is made to
say: ". . . I wonder that strangers and uncircumsized and
idol-worshippers have been converted and have entered
into the promises of God, but Israel has not entered.
. . ."[3] This Christianized Moses and the emotional
Gregory had numerous counterparts throughout the
earlier Middle Ages, but it was not until the end of the
eleventh century that feeling and wonder gave way to
rioting and violence directed at Jewish communities.
R. W. Southern suggests that the new, awakening spirit
of critical inquiry, as it began to investigate the premises
of the Christian religion, its credibility, and its truth,
encountered the distinct and alien Jews: "Scattered
throughout Europe in considerable numbers, and enjoy-
ing a level of prosperity and intellectual culture far
above the average, were communities of Jews, testifying
that [the Christian religion] was not true."[4] Thus Jewish criticism of the Incarnation inspires the schoolman
Anselm to write his *Cur Deus Homo*, while other Christian apologists answer other unbelievers.[5] Anselm's use
of dialectic and his reliance on rational argument are a
landmark in human thought; nevertheless the results of
this disputation hardly need elaboration. Some three
hundred years later William Langland respected the
people of Abraham and the law of Moses and yet railed
at the Jews for their continuing disbelief. Langland's
more famous contemporary, Chaucer, wrote a tale about
ritual murder that, even if interpreted as a kind of romance or saint's life, presents the same problems as do
the characters Shylock and Fagin.

While no one can indeed ever forget all these things,
it was not primarily to recall them that the Center for
Medieval and Early Renaissance Studies at SUNY-Bing-

hamton chose to devote its Eighth Annual Conference (3–5 May 1974) to *Jewish Culture in the Middle Ages*. As in its previous conferences, the Fellows of the Center sought to give wide disciplinary coverage to a general topic for an audience of medievalists from various disciplines and backgrounds. There was no intention to exhaust the possibilities of so large a topic in a conference not quite two days long, for such an intention is patent folly. Rather there was the felt need to allow established and innovative scholars the opportunity to present a contemporary treatment of Jews in the Middle Ages that, though not suppressing the implications of majority history, would develop in general medievalists some knowledge of the deep and rich culture of the Jewish community. There was the further hope that the development of an increased awareness would avoid the patronizing pitfall of the "contributions" topos; as Yosef H. Yerushalmi notes (p. 21): "Medieval Jews did not awake each day to ponder—'what shall I contribute today?' Nor did they generally conceive of themselves as impresarios of cultural contact, the Sol Huroks of the Middle Ages." To begin to accomplish the large purpose of the conference, which would hopefully continue long after it was over, the conference program had to consider the general relationship of Jewish studies to medieval studies as well as specific topics within fields. The program took the following shape:

Yosef H. Yerushalmi on the relationship between Jewish studies and medieval studies

Rosemary Radford Ruether on the patristic basis for Christian attitudes on the Jews

Harriet Goldberg on the Hispanic literary tradition

Norman Stillman on Jewish Spain

Josef Gutmann on problems in Jewish art

> Leslie Fiedler on myth criticism and medieval stud-
> ies
>
> *Disputatio* with Edward A. Synan, Jeremy duQ.
> Adams, Norman Cantor, Alice Colby-Hall,
> Stanley Ferber

Two major papers on Spain represented a logical emphasis on an important area in Jewish history. The *Disputatio* was an innovation in the CEMERS Conference
format, intended to give an active conclusion to the program and to provide an analysis, criticism, and summary
of the proceedings.

Jeremy duQ. Adams's perception that "the extraordinary variety of discourse—of styles and genres as well
as individual addresses—(p. 174)" was both a pleasure
and a problem reflects the fundamental difficulty in
planning any program that is "interdisciplinary." In
Confessions XI.xiv, Augustine comments about time:
"What then is time? If no one asks me, I know; if I
want to explain it to a questioner, I do not know;"[6]
would that scholars have the same certain uncertainty
about the idea "interdisciplinary." Despite many calls
for interdisciplinary studies and many large grants for
such activities, it is hard to see how this vogue term has
specific content and how scholarship can be interdisciplinary in a primary sense. A case in point is the widely
divergent intellectual viewpoints of Yerushalmi and
Fiedler. When Yerushalmi insists upon a close scrutiny
of original sources, his is the position of a thorough,
careful historian. Fiedler can hardly be more different.
Espousing a literary point of view that allows the critic
to be as important as the thing criticized, Fiedler attempts to go beyond the facts of the twelfth century to
find meaning in the Grail legend. Those who wish may
consult Philip Rahv's essay on the enmity between his-

tory and myth, wherein they will find a clear and deep analysis of this fundamental opposition.[7] Such a tension between the disciplines, duplicated in major and minor points and complicated by various interpretations within a discipline, has to force in an attentive audience an awareness of the interdisciplinary perspective. This fusion in the generalist audience may so far be the closest approximation to interdisciplinary activity that American scholarship may attain. Adams's closing suggestion in his critique that structuralism may be the answer provides a tempting, though as yet unproven, prospect. As to "interdisciplinary" in the secondary sense, i.e., the sum of disparate disciplinary parts, the program surely qualifies by virtue of its "extraordinary variety of discourse."

Thus Yerushalmi speaks for the Fellows of the Center when he extends an open invitation to general medievalists to study medieval Jewry in order to continue the writing of a truly universal history and to participate in the illumination of the human condition through such history. His broad appeal is a logical result of his survey of "Medieval Jewry: From Within and From Without." Yerushalmi establishes that scholarly neglect of medieval Jewry derives from the earliest centuries of Christianity. Up to the nineteenth century the virtually consistent theme was that the Jews had no history. Whatever interest there might have been was antiquarian or conversionist. With the development of history as a discipline in the nineteenth century Yerushalmi sees the beginning of a significant departure from a majority, triumphalist treatment of the Jews. This *Wissenschaft des Judentums*, characterized by a proliferation of books and the founding of several important periodicals, nevertheless did not convince the universities to recognize postbiblical Judaism as a distinct discipline. Such recognition came after World War I, along with wider acceptance of scholarly work on Jewish culture by university presses and generalist periodicals. Yerushalmi, however, is not willing to see this century as a golden age of Jewish studies. Except for research in Spain, he finds a still widespread reluctance to overcome linguistic obstacles, to review limited historical categories, and to reconsider canonized stereotypes. The integral view of medieval Jewish history will elude twentieth century scholarship unless the medievalist goes to archival material and to Jewish sources for the reconstruction of Jewish history and culture. Even well-prepared with a knowledge of original sources, the historian must avoid the "contributions" topos, the misplaced emphasis on Jewish sources as merely a mine of general information, facile parallels, expiatory *leidengeschichte*, and the currently popular stereotypes of alienation. In short, the historian and the medievalist must be willing to free themselves from preconceptions inherited or contemporary.

Rosemary Radford Ruether develops in detail one of the major points that Yerushalmi raises by investigating the nature and meaning of the *Adversus Judaeos* tradition. This broad category of writings includes testimonies, treatises, sermons, and dialogues that formed the attitude of the Christian community towards Jews living after Christ and towards the Jewish nation before Christ. When Constantine made Christianity the official religion of the Roman Empire, the ideas in these works helped define the legal status of the Jews in the Christian state. Ruether groups the anti-Jewish themes in the *Adversus Judaeos* writings into two general types. The first stresses the rejection of the Jews and the election of the Gentiles, while the second emphasizes the inferiority of the Jewish law and cult and the true spiritual fulfillment of Christianity. The rejection of Christ as the Messiah is the central act of perfidy, but for many Fathers of the Church this rejection is part of a long heritage of refusing to heed the prophets. At every point in their history the Jews manifest their perversity in doing whatever God does not want them to do. Even before Christ's coming there existed two people, namely, the evil, sinning Jews, and the faithful heroes and prophets who were the precursors of the Church. The concept of two nations finds its expression in Christian exegesis of Ishmael and Isaac, Jacob and Esau, Cain and Abel, Sarah and Hagar, etc. Ruether considers the climactic theme of this tradition to be the Christian belief that the reprobation of the Jews is permanent and irrevocable. The Temple destroyed and the Nation scattered, the Jews must live in bondage under divine wrath until the end of time. Christianity is the eschatological Israel. Thus in dividing Time at the birth of Christ Christianity creates a dualistic perspective wherein the Jews receive the negative side of every dualism. Ruether concludes with the observation that cultural obliteration of Jewish history is "programmed" into Christianity. From her perspective it is necessary for contemporary Christianity to acknowledge this history of dualisms not as a problem of external community relations, but rather as an internal problem coming from the theology of messianic fulfillment. Christianity must reexamine Christology itself. The tone and substance of these conclusions put Ruether in disagreement with Yerushalmi's *caveat* against expiatory *leidengeschichte*. In the *Disputatio* Adams takes significant exception to a number of points Ruether makes on patristic authors and suggests that in some ways Ruether overstates her case.

The polemics of theological debate need not correspond with historic reality. In "Aspects of Jewish Life

in Islamic Spain" Norman Stillman sketches that reality
in the so-called Golden Age. Though somewhat less
exuberant and more cautious than a number of his
scholarly predecessors, Stillman finds much to praise in
Spain of the tenth to twelfth centuries. It is not surprising that there might have been a cultural efflorescence
during this period, since there is clear evidence of a
Jewish presence in Roman times and some suggestion of
even earlier Jewish activity. During the earlier Arabic
rule Jews seem to have been a relatively well-assimilated
minority. Like their Muslim counterparts, the Jews
looked eastward for their religious and cultural inspiration. When Andalusia became an independent caliphate,
however, Spanish Jewry began to flourish on its own.
Stillman attributes the rise of the Jewish community to
its leader, Hasday b. Shaprut. Physician, statesman, patron, Hasday saw Spain as the leading seat of Spanish
Jewry and thus broke with the Jews of Baghdad, who
had formerly been the authority for most Jews in the
Islamic world. The poetry of this period, refined and
sensual, not only gives evidence of the thorough Jewish
assimilation of the Islamic milieu, but also reflects the
same cultural concerns of the Hispano-Arabic society.
The powerful Samuel ha-Nagid exemplifies for Stillman the upper-class pride in language, lineage, and religion which he finds characteristic of Andalusian Jewry. The Nagid even wrote a polemical treatise exposing
the inconsistencies of the Koran without any reprisal.
The close connection between politics and culture that
promoted Jewish culture, however, eventually dimin-
ished it. The decline created a spiritual crisis that ani-
mates many of Judah ha-Levi's poems. In *The Kuzari*
ha-Levi virtually equates the pride of Andalusian Jewry
with vanity. He sought his consolation in Palestine;

some thirty years later the Golden Age was over.

Harriet Goldberg's paper on antifeminism and anti-semitism further extends the patristic studies of Ruether and provides a kind of reversal and complement to Stillman's description of the Golden Age by showing how later Spanish writers saw stereotypes in history rather than gold. Goldberg succinctly presents her thesis with the rhetorical question: "Is it necessary to establish to any reader of patristic or exemplary literature that the Church had two enemies or adversaries besides Satan—women and the Jews?" (p. 87) She assembles evidence to show that Spanish writers depict each group as lascivious, treacherous, and demonic. Biblical texts, patristic writing, marriage laws, and vernacular treatises state or imply that the Jew is a sexual peril, just as similar works argue that woman is a threat to celibacy, abstinence, and temperance. Numerous passages also treat Jews and women as betrayers. Some sources, e.g., blame the Jews for the treachery that made the Arab invasion of 711 possible, while others hold women accountable. Jews and women are furthermore magicians and witches who show they are the Devil's minions by their arts as well as by their devilish pride. The parallels converge in one anecdote about a Jewish woman who, unable to provide milk for her son during the siege of Jerusalem, satisfies her own hunger by roasting him. "Never were you more sweet to me my son," she says as she offers various parts to others. Such an outrageous story recalls Marlowe's Barabbas and, to a lesser degree, Shylock. Unlike T. S. Eliot, who sees such characterizations as the savage comic humor of farce and would no doubt say the same for this anecdote, Goldberg chooses a more current mode of interpretation in concluding that Jews and women were the alien out-

siders who threatened the ethical structure and the outcasts who *were* assigned the sins the community feared
most.[8]

The last two papers on the program depart from a
concern with history, culture, and stereotype to consider
the problematic in the fine arts. Josef Gutmann addresses a number of related problems in the controversies surrounding the interpretation of medieval Jewish
art. While he points out that scholars who argue that
the Second Commandment effectively prohibited Jewish
art assume that Judaism was static and monolithic, he is
not quick to go to the other extreme of positing a flourishing Jewish art that was the source of Old Testament
Christian art. The Dura-Europos cycle, often cited as
evidence for antecedent illustrated manuscript cycles,
more likely descends from pattern or model books. Gutmann grants that Jewish legend and lore were the literary sources for many extrabiblical themes and motifs,
such as Abraham's repudiation of idol worship and his
subsequent clash with Nimrod. Iconography and style
in the three religions are so diverse that the claim of
common descent is untenable. In the Middle Ages there
was, however, a Jewish iconography that was distinct
from Christian iconography, but without a unique style.
Hebrew manuscripts from Germany, for example, depict
conceptions of Jewish afterlife, specifically the messianic banquet. These later medieval manuscripts treat a
unique Jewish theme, even though the cosmic beasts
they present derive from the bestiaries. Thus close and
careful examination can allow one to accept the ideas
that there was Jewish influence on art and that there was
Jewish artistic expression.

Leslie Fiedler's discussion of Chrétien de Troyes's
Perceval and the background of the Grail legend locates
a Jewish core and meaning in one of the basic myths of

the West. Fiedler suggests that the Grail legend is the complement and binary opposite of the story of Oedipus, thus a Jewish antithesis to a Greek thesis. So archetypal and so fundamental a significance no doubt explains its enduring appeal through the Renaissance and its later rebirth in the Romantic era. The scholarly search for sources appears to be an ironic continuation of the legend, if not a quixotic quest, but Fiedler himself searches for the Jewish connection. Perceval is the inarticulate *schlemiehl* who kills his mother by leaving home and who restores sexual potency to his father. As the lineal descendant of Joseph of Arimathea, Perceval's Jewish heritage is clear. The Grail Castle, which many scholars see as a replica of the Temple, is moreover the scene of a Grail ceremony resembling the orthodox Passover Seder. The Jewishness of the Grail legend and yet the antisemitic tonalities of Chrétien's work have a complementary meaning in the light of Bernard's seventy-ninth sermon, where Bernard calls Israel the mother of Christianity. If Chrétien labels the Jews killers of God, then Bernard implies that Christians are matricides for abandoning the Synagogue. Despite his plea for charity at the beginning of *Perceval* Chrétien denies charity to Israel; consequently with Perceval he kills the Mother who had given birth to those who seek *caritas*.

The presentation of the *Disputatio* in published form poses a number of editorial problems that recall the Watergate affair. The printed record herein derives from tapes of an essentially spontaneous interaction between the disputants, who had seen first drafts of the papers, and the lecturers, who could only anticipate possible criticisms. It may be a violation of a quasi-Jeffersonian principle ("that editor edits best who edits least"), but each participant had an opportunity to review the raw transcript of the tapes and to make stylistic, but hopefully not substantive, changes for the printed version. Otherwise readers might have found it necessary to pursue some of the more difficult aspects of discourse analysis. As it is, much of the colloquial flavor of the interchanges remains in syntax and idiom. The essential intellectual substance of the event should still confront the reader. Adams's wide-ranging critique, Cantor's aggressive call for subversive history, Colby-Hall's gracious but precise queries, and Ferber's light but serious synagogic response answer the prepared papers directly, if not bluntly at times. In the ultimate sense the printed version cannot be the tapes, which cannot be the event itself, but Father Synan's "Afterwords," written a few months later, aptly summarizes the *Disputatio* and the entire conference as they must now appear to participant and reader. And so it goes.

I must thank several people who have made this volume and the conference possible. Dorothy Huber, the Center secretary, organized many of the details of the conference and showed her great patience with the tapes and the volume's editor. Charles Lansdown, president of the Medieval and Renaissance Society, and his associates solved every minor crisis during the two days of the conference. Allan Eller spent many hours helping in the preparation of the manuscript. François Bucher, codirector of the Center, did much of the original planning. Bernard F. Huppé, codirector, freely gave his experience and encouragement.

NOTES

1. Gregory the Great, "Tenth Homily on the Gospels," PL 76, 1111:

To be sure all the elements gave witness that their
Author had come. Let me say something about them
in a human way: the heavens acknowledged that he
was God because they immediately sent a star. The
sea acknowledged him because it made itself the
shoes for the soles of his feet. The earth acknowledged him because it trembled when he was dying.
The sun acknowledged him because it hid the rays
of its light. Rocks and walls recognized him because
they fell to pieces at the times of his death. Hell
acknowledged him because it returned the dead
whom it held. Nevertheless, the hearts of the still
faithless Jews by no means recognize him as God
whom all the unfeeling elements perceived as Lord,
and, harder than rock, they are unwilling to be cleft
to repentance, and him they deny to confess Whom
the elements, as we said, were acclaiming as God
either by miracles or by breaking into pieces.

2. Aelfric, *The Homilies of the Anglo-Saxon Church*,
   ed. B. Thorpe (London, 1844–46) I, p. 108.

3. *Vision of St. Paul*, tr. Andrew Rutherford, in *The
   Ante-Nicene Fathers* (New York, 1908) IX, p. 164.

4. R. W. Southern, *Medieval Humanism and Other
   Studies* (Oxford, 1970), p. 11.

5. R. W. Southern, *Saint Anselm and His Biographer*
   (Cambridge, 1963), Chapter III "Cur Deus Homo,"
   pp. 77–121, but especially pp. 88–91.

6. Augustine, *The Confessions*, tr. F. J. Sheed (New
   York, 1943), p. 271.

7. Philip Rahv, "The Myth and the Powerhouse," in
   the collection by the same title, (New York, 1953),
   pp. 3–21.

8. See Eliot's essay on "Christopher Marlowe," in his
   Selected Essays (London, 1949), p. 123.

MEDIEVAL JEWRY:

FROM WITHIN AND

FROM WITHOUT*

Yosef Hayim Yerushalmi

Under ordinary and more prosaic circumstances I should
have delivered a limited substantive paper on some
particular aspect of my work, preferably one so arcane
as to be immune to criticism. However your invitation
to deliver an opening address, as well as the occasion
itself, have moved me to extend both my perimeters and
vulnerabilities to larger issues, and thus to appear more
exuberantly *engagé* than is my custom. In the time at
my disposal I shall necessarily have to simplify a number of complexities, for which I beg your indulgence.

Briefly stated, my central theses are the following:

*This paper having been conceived and delivered as a public
address, I have refrained from altering its immediate "oral"
character in sending it off to the press. For the same reason I
have not seen fit to encumber the text with footnotes. For those
who desire comprehensive bibliographic information on any
aspect of medieval Jewish studies the following, above all, are
to be recommended: Shlomo Shunami, *Bibliography of Jewish
Bibliographies*, 2nd ed. (Jerusalem, 1969); Salo W. Baron, *A
Social and Religious History of the Jews*, 2nd rev. ed., 15 vols.
(New York, 1952 et seq.); and the collaborative volume *Bibliographic Essays in Medieval Jewish Studies* (New York, 1976).

First—That the widespread neglect by general medievalists of the Jewish component in medieval history is due in large measure to inherited, though often unconscious and culturally metamorphosed, theological and ideological biases.

Second—That even when medievalists do turn their attention to medieval Jewry they are constrained, by their equipment and the sources accessible to them, to view the Jews in an essentially external manner. Their conception of medieval Jewry is thus not only limited but, by that very token, also distorted.

Third—That there are compelling reasons as to why this situation should change.

And now, if you will allow a Jewish historian an alien metaphor, the rest of this address will consist of an attempt to nail these theses to the door.

1

We shall begin at the point of origins.

Western conceptions of Jewish history trail an exceedingly long pedigree. Indeed the fundamental attitudes were already forged in the very earliest centuries of Christianity and remained surprisingly consistent down to modern times.

As the Incarnation was seen to bisect all historical time, so, in the Christian schema, the Crucifixion split Jewish history into two radically disparate segments. Placed on one side was the biblical history of Israel, God's chosen people. This history was sacred and supremely meaningful, so much so that it was appropriated now as the prehistory of Christendom itself. In the "New Israel" which supersedes the "Old" in the eyes of God, biblical history is to find its direct continuity and fulfillment, while, conversely, the subsequent history of the Jews themselves is deflected to the side. Indeed the postbiblical history of the rejected people turns out upon examination to be no history at all. It may be more adequately described as an implacable existential curse to be endured by the Jews to the end of time.

What the Gospels adumbrated, the Church Fathers elaborated and systematized. Already prior to Constantine, but in an accelerating crescendo thereafter, Christian triumphalism was nowhere more insistent and strident than in its polemics against the Jews. Without pausing to consider the irony of such a position, those who spoke in the name of a crucified messiah saw nothing inconsistent in exploiting the visible historical defeat of the Jewish people to the full. The loss of kingdom and Temple, the political subjugation of the Jews throughout their global exile, were primary proofs to demonstrate the Christian claim against them. Postbiblical Jewish history was denuded of any positive value except as witness to Christian victory in the world. The Jews have nothing more to say, unless it be to bemoan their condition, nothing further to do but persist helplessly in a state of negative suspension until the Second Coming shall precipitate their final conversion. Postbiblical Jewish history (if such it can still be called) is thus completely static. Apprehended in such terms it is, we must repeat, no history at all.

That such inherited views remained dominant in the Middle Ages is surely too obvious to require extended discussion. I only want to stress that the problem, of course, does not lie in the absence of actual chronicles devoted to postbiblical Jewish history. To expect such writings from medieval Christians would be absurd (though, as we shall see, it becomes less so when we enter the period from the sixteenth to the eighteenth centuries). Even among the Jews themselves, prior to a sudden surge of historiography in the sixteenth century, historical chronicles are few and far between. But the relative neglect of explicitly historical writings by medieval Jews certainly had nothing to do with an acceptance of Christian verdicts. Jews, for example, had no doubt whatever that biblical and postbiblical Judaism form a seamless whole and that they are not only the physical but the spiritual heirs of their biblical ancestors. If historiography was not cultivated by them *per se*, all genres of medieval Jewish literature, whether legal, exegetical, philosophical, or mystical, are replete with richly varied attitudes toward history and speculations as to the nature of Jewish historical destinies.

On the other hand, no matter to what genre we turn among medieval Christians, whenever Jews are discussed the patristic image of them remains so ingrained as to preclude, *ab initio*, any consideration of the Jews as a serious factor in history. This point must be formulated and understood with precision. It means, in essence, that the role of spectator assigned the Jews amid the flux of history was not even necessarily an empirical conclusion derived from the realities of their position among the nations. Being axiomatic to begin with, it did not have to be deduced. If you require a vivid symbol that compresses everything succinctly, you may have it in the Crusades. Throughout the Crusades, and the even longer history of the crusading idea in Europe, Jerusalem is regarded as an issue between Christendom and Islam alone. It is so not only politically and militarily, but above all psychologically. Upon the outermost horizons of the crusading mentality the very question of any Jewish stake in the fate of the Holy City could not possibly impinge—not because there were no Jews in Palestine (there were), nor because Jews were indifferent to the outcome of the struggle (on the contrary, they were often actively concerned), but rather because the nexus between the Jews and Jerusalem was regarded as irrevocably ruptured in the year 70, and the issue settled for all time. It was, after all, not until 1967 that the world was rudely awakened to the unanticipated vista of Jews guarding the Church of the Holy Sepulchre and the Mosque of Omar.

2

Lest one be tempted to ascribe medieval attitudes merely to ignorance of postbiblical Judaism, let it be noted that the development of Christian Hebraism from the Renaissance and Reformation through the eighteenth century brought no significant change. In the first place, the interest was in postbiblical Judaism, not in postbiblical Jews. Indeed, except in one vital respect (conversion), its motives were largely unrelated to an understanding of the Jews. Various aspects of rabbinic and medieval Jewish literature were studied, major texts were rendered into Latin for a variety of reasons. Beginning already in the thirteenth century and continually thereafter, Talmud and Midrash had been ransacked for evidence in favor of Christianity and for materials for ridicule and vituperation. During the Renaissance the Kabbalah was suddenly unveiled and interpreted as an esoteric quasi-Christian tradition within the bosom of Judaism which allegedly confirmed the Christian truth. In the seventeenth and eighteenth centuries Christian Hebraists began to investigate rabbinic literature for philological purposes, for archaeological data on ancient Palestine, or for the elucidation of Christian Scripture. Serious attention was paid to some of the medieval Jewish biblical commentators. Monumental bibliographies, such as those of Giulio Bartolocci and Johann Christoph Wolf, covered the entire range of Jewish literature since the Bible with a thoroughness and erudition that make them useful tools to this day. The number of postbiblical Jewish works available in translation grew steadily. Some of what had been accomplished by the eighteenth century can be seen conveniently assembled in the great *Thesaurus antiquitatum sacrarum* of Blaisio Ugolino. Published in Venice between 1744 and 1769, this anthology of Latin translations of Jewish texts runs to no less than thirty-four folio volumes.

It is therefore all the more instructive to observe the degree to which Christian Hebraists were able mentally to divorce the texts they studied from the actual bearers of the tradition which these same texts represented. With very few exceptions these scholars turn out to have been either overtly hostile to Jews, indifferent to their fate, or interested in them largely as objects for polemics and conversion, with the last type predominating by far.

Little wonder, perhaps, that despite all this protracted activity, extending over several centuries, there was little interest in the history of the Jews since their dispersion. A Jewish historical text was occasionally translated, but otherwise the emphasis was either conversionist or antiquarian. Only one man, the Huguenot pastor Jacques Basnage, a refugee from France residing in the Netherlands, became somehow sufficiently interested in the later history of the Jews to attempt to narrate it. His pioneering *Histoire des juifs depuis Jésus-Christ jusqu'à présent* was published in seven volumes in 1706–11 and in an expanded fifteen-volume edition in 1716–26. But Basnage is merely the striking exception that confirms the rule. Even so the final chapter of the fifteenth volume is entitled: "Diverses remarques sur la conversion des juifs."

Christian Hebraists were generally believing Christians, bound, we would say, by theological presuppositions. We would perhaps expect novelties from the men of the Enlightenment. But while the erosion of the Christian historical framework and of European insularity created a new receptivity for the history of Muslims and Chinese, it did not accomplish the same for that of the Jews. No real interest in Jewish history was generated during the Enlightenment, though this did not inhibit various *philosophes* from expressing quite definite opinions concerning the Jews and their character. If there was an innovation, it lay in the fact that now, for good measure, even biblical history was derogated. Voltaire's antisemitism, much discussed and debated in recent years, as well as that of other Enlightenment figures, need not detain us here. Diderot's ability to attack the Inquisition throughout his career without ever mentioning the crypto-Jews of Spain and Portugal, who were its primary victims, is interesting, but by no means unique. The real issue lies elsewhere, in the inability of the Enlightenment to concede a place to the Jews *as Jews* within its notions of universal history. At their most favorable, some of the currents in the Enlightenment held out a possibility for a time when the Jews shall have become "men." Not the Jewish past of the Jews, but their assimilated un-Jewish future is the focus of attention and a leitmotif in all arguments for toleration. In the grand debates that preceded Jewish emancipation in France, the staunchest advocates of the Jewish cause could see nothing positive in the history of the Jews. For these advocates it was nothing but an unrelieved tale of persecution and decadence, and if they invoked Jewish history, it was only to blame it for the more unpleasant qualities of contemporary Jews which their adversaries regarded as innate. In the end, whether it was the Jews who had corrupted their own history, as their opponents claimed, or their history that had corrupted the Jews, as their friends maintained, one result was the same. Viewed in this way, Jewish history could at best evoke pity. It could not possibly be a subject deserving the attention of serious and rational men.

3

In the nineteenth century history came into its own as an autonomous discipline and, for better or worse, the historian's profession as we know it was born.

Something else occurred in the process. Potentially, at least, and increasingly in practice, historiography now claimed within its province all of man's past and the past of all men. No period could be considered too remote, no culture too exotic (indeed, no subject too obscure) for historical investigation. If so, why not the history of the Jews as well?

There were signs of budding interest. In 1821, for example, the Académie Royale in Paris offered a prize for a work describing the condition of the Jews in medieval France. Then too the agitated question of Jewish emancipation in Germany and elsewhere prompted a certain attention to the legal status of Jews in the various countries during the Middle Ages and sometimes led to the publication of relevant documents. Articles dealing with aspects of medieval Jewish history occasionally made their appearance in scholarly journals. Yet any survey of the contribution of general medievalists in the nineteenth century to the study of medieval

Jewry would easily reveal how peripheral the matter of the Jews remained.

Major historians mentioned the Jews, if at all, only in passing, and usually in connection with moneylending or some other "unsavory" economic role which made them appear as sporadic and unwelcome intruders into the authentic history of the nation. The relatively few studies devoted explicitly to medieval Jewry were themselves almost always ancillary outgrowths of work done in other fields such as legal and institutional history, Church history, or local and provincial history. Leaving aside such amateur works as Miss Hanna Adams's *History of the Jews from the Destruction of Jerusalem to the Nineteenth Century* (Boston, 1812), or the *History of the Jews from the Earliest Period down to Modern Times* produced in England in 1830 by Henry Hart Milman, later dean of St. Paul's, one is hard put to find any attempts by professional historians to write Jewish history of any scope. George Depping's *Les juifs dans le moyen-âge* of 1834 was an expansion of his work on medieval French Jewry which had won an honorable mention in the Paris competition of 1821. In Holland, Hendrik Koenen published a serviceable *Geschiedenis der Joden in Nederland* in 1843, the first history of Dutch Jewry. Otto Stobbe's classic work, *Die Juden in Deutschland während des Mittelalters*, published in 1866, was a comprehensive study of Jewish status by a great historian of medieval German law. In a different class is Gustave Saige's *Les juifs du Languedoc* (1888), which, being the work of an archivist, is in the documentary tradition of the École des Chartes. In any case these works, with their variety of purposes and quality, and the few others one could muster, stand out as solitary examples amid the general indifference. To be sure, nineteenth-century historiography began with an emphasis on political history, which may have contributed to the neglect of the history of a people that had been stateless for almost two millenia. But this factor was only subsidiary. Beneath the surface lay the dual heritage of Christian and rationalist derogations of Jewish history, to which were actively joined the more modern national and racial prejudices against Jews which were as rampant in academic circles as in society at large. The works we have mentioned cannot obscure the fact that throughout the nineteenth century, except for the biblical period, it was left to the Jews to write their own history.

And so they did. Beginning in Germany in the 1820s, and later elsewhere, a new type of learning gained momentum in the midst of Jewry. They called it *Wissenschaft des Judentums*, a phrase best translated as "the scientific study of the Jewish past." Its avowed premise lay in the dispassionate application of the critical methodology and techniques of German historical scholarship to Jewish sources. Its motives were more complex. They included a desire to discover historically what Judaism was, now that modern life had shattered the old consensus; to reveal the Jewish past to alienated Jewish intellectuals; to advance the cause of Jewish emancipation by exposing historical lies and myths about the Jews.

In retrospect, therefore, the essential miracle of nineteenth-century *Wissenschaft des Judentums* lies in the extent and solidity of the achievement despite the built-in hazards of intramural discourse, ideology, and apologetics, to which it sometimes succumbed. I shall not attempt to catalogue for you the veritable library of historical scholarship that was produced. It will suffice to observe that the *Monatsschrift für Geschichte und Wis-*

senschaft des Judentums (founded in 1852 and forced to discontinue only in the dark year of 1939) or the *Revue des études juives* (established in Paris in 1880 and, after an interruption in World War II, still issued today) would have no difficulty in holding their own when placed beside the *Historische Zeitschrift* or the *Revue historique*.

And yet the cumulative results of decades of intensive Jewish scholarship were virtually without influence upon general historiography. The isolated position of *Wissenschaft des Judentums* paralleled the peculiar plight of the scholars who labored to create it. These men received their general historical and philological training at the universities. But they were aware from the beginning that they could not hope for a university career in their chosen field, for postbiblical Judaica was never admitted to the universities as a recognized and distinct discipline. Fragments were occasionally dispersed among other fields, such as Semitic philology, and on principle these were not taught by Jews. The Judaic scholar had the option of being a rabbi or a librarian, teaching on the elementary or middle level, or, in the most favorable instance, holding a professorship at one of the few modern Jewish theological seminaries in the various European countries. Whatever the choice, it meant that he did his work beyond the pale of the university. When in 1894 the Prussian government was finally moved to recognize the phenomenal achievements of the seventy-seven-year-old Moritz Steinschneider, the "Nestor of Hebrew bibliography," it awarded him the honorary title of "Professor." The director of the Royal Library personally delivered the diploma to his home. It was not bestowed in a formal public ceremony at the University of Berlin where, needless to say, he had never been offered an actual teaching position.

The incident is, in its way, paradigmatic for an entire century. By its close historians had extended their vistas of the past far beyond those available to any previous age. And yet vis-à-vis the Jews, history remained what it had been since the Church Fathers—triumphalist, majority history, in which the Jew was either absent or alien.

4

It cannot be denied that on certain levels significant developments have taken place in our own century. Foremost, certainly, is the entry of postbiblical Judaica into the universities. My own university was the first to do so. Yet one is sobered by the realization that Harvard's Littauer Professorship of Hebrew Literature and Philosophy, the oldest in the world, was established as late as 1925, to be followed in 1930 by Columbia's Miller chair in Jewish History, Literature and Institutions. The enormous prestige of the longtime incumbents of these two chairs, Harry Austryn Wolfson and Salo Wittmayer Baron, retrospectively had much to do with the subsequent recognition of postbiblical Judaica in the academic community at large. Still for many years these remained the only such professorships in the country. It is really since the end of World War II, and especially within the last decade, that various branches of Judaica have proliferated on American campuses to the degree that the demand now far exceeds the number of qualified candidates.

Parallel to this have been the effects of the Jewish national renaissance in Israel. In a famous passage in *Émile* Jean Jacques Rousseau had written: "I shall believe I have really heard the reports of the Jews only when they have a free state, schools, universities, where they can speak and dispute without risk. Then we shall know what they have to say." That vision found its fulfillment with the establishment of the Hebrew University in Jerusalem at the outset of the British Mandate and, of late, with the universities of Tel Aviv, Bar Ilan, Haifa, and Beer Sheba. At all these Israeli seats of learning research in medieval Jewish history is actively pursued in all its ramified areas. Whether the reports have really been heard is a question to which we shall return.

Another landmark of sorts was reached in the *Cambridge Medieval History*, begun in 1911. Six volumes appeared with only sparse and scattered references to Jews. Suddenly, in the seventh volume, devoted to the fourteenth century and published in 1932, medieval Jewish history came into its own with an entire chapter. It was written by the late Cecil Roth, then Reader in Jewish studies at Oxford. In an assignment which, despite its assurance of immortality, few would envy, he managed to compress fourteen centuries of Jewish history, from the Roman dispersion to 1492, into thirty pages. The dual significance of the event should not be missed. On the one hand, medieval Jewry was thus granted a recognition it had rarely, if ever, received before. On the other, the whole of medieval Jewry was placed in splendid isolation, immured between a chapter on "Russia, 1015–1462," and another entitled "Medieval Estates." In the *Cambridge Medieval History* the chapter on the Jews is, in effect, a historiographical ghetto.

Much more, certainly, has changed in recent years. The Judaic scholar is suddenly no longer an orphan. His work, if it is good (and sometimes when it is not), finds ready access to scholarly journals and university presses. A recent issue of the *American Historical Review* not only contained two articles touching on medieval Jewry, but actually boasted a picture of a medieval Jew on the cover—a sign, some would say, that he had finally "arrived." I shall not attempt to document further the various indications of rising interest. This conference is itself a confirmation of it.

Yet when all is said and done, and for all the flurries of attention, it is doubtful that even today most general medievalists possess anything that approaches an integral view of medieval Jewish history.

I shall not concern myself with the outright bias of commission or omission that continues to plague most books on medieval history when it comes to the Jews. That task has already been performed by Gavin Langmuir of Stanford in a careful and eloquent study of "Majority History and Post-Biblical Jews" published in 1966 in the *Journal of the History of Ideas*, which I heartily recommend to all. I have rather in mind those medievalists, be they in history or literature, with a serious interest in medieval Jewry or an incipient desire even to direct some of their own research toward medieval Jewish topics.

The most telling fact is that these do not even know the language (or languages) of the Jews, and there is not the vaguest indication of a trend to acquire them. It is a state of affairs almost inconceivable in any other field. Granted, medieval Hebrew is not an easy language. All the earlier layers and resonances are alive in it. Moreover many medieval Jewish texts are written in a Hebrew interwoven with Talmudic Aramaic and in a style for whose understanding some actual Talmudic study is often the best preparation.

Yet one takes many pains for scholarship. For the study of Gnosticism Greek and Latin are no longer ade-

quate today, and so Germans, Frenchmen, and bonafide
Anglo-Saxons study Coptic and Mongolian. The British,
whose mispronunciation of foreign tongues might seem
almost a phonetic xenophobia, have long produced
some of the most distinguished Arabists in the world.
One afternoon some time ago a vivacious young Italian
woman from the University of Turin was introduced to
an incredulous Eliot House Common Room as—*mira-
bile dictu*—a specialist in seventeenth-century American
Puritan literature.

It is only in speaking of medieval Jewry that scholars
seem somehow exempt from a linguistic obligation
which is admitted as basic anywhere else if one is to be
taken seriously. In this respect the radical decline since
the seventeenth and eighteenth centuries deserves attention. As we have seen, in that earlier period substantial
numbers of non-Jewish scholars were able to handle
Talmudic and medieval Jewish sources; among contemporary medievalists they are hardly to be found. If,
fortunately, the missionary thrust of scholarship has
been abandoned, so, alas, has knowledge of postbiblical
Hebrew. Nor does modern Hebrew fare better, and
therefore the bulk of medieval scholarship in Israel remains unknown to medievalists elsewhere.

The only country to which these remarks do not apply
is Spain. There a number of historical and ideological
circumstances have combined, since the nineteenth century, not only to generate unusual interest in medieval
Jewish history, but to produce a fairly impressive roster
of scholars capable of studying that history from original inner sources. These scholars, many of whom command both medieval and modern Hebrew, are grouped
around the Instituto Arias Montano in Madrid and
Barcelona. Since 1940 the Instituto has published, besides a large series of texts and studies, one of the most

important scholarly journals in Judaica to be found anywhere. It is entitled *Sefarad*, the Hebrew name for
Spain. Despite certain limitations and slants, Spain remains the only European country in which the record of
medieval Jewry is claimed somehow as an organic part
of the national patrimony, and only there do we find
scholars who are able to explore the Jewish materials at
firsthand. But then Spain, as everyone knows, is a peculiar place. Elsewhere, be it in Europe or America,
Hebrew is simply not part of the medievalist's equipment. As a result the inner life of medieval Jewry is virtually closed to him.

5

The difficulties are compounded by other considerations.
In essence, none of the available categories established
in the conceptualization of general history will neatly
accommodate the Jews in the Middle Ages or do justice
to their experience. Not *Sektengeschichte*, for they were
not a sect, nor *Religionsgeschichte*, for obviously they
were much more than a religion. A nation? Yes, but
surely not in the ordinary sense. How elusive of the
Jews.

Nor will currently canonized stereotypes or sociological "models" help much as one gropes toward historical
realities. In a global and millennial dispersion, which
Jew are you talking about? The one with the Jewish
badge and the meek expression on the cover of the
American Historical Review? If so, when and where?
"Ghetto-dweller?" But stone walls, of themselves, do
not a ghetto make. The enforced ghetto is a phenomenon and hallmark of early modern times, from the sixteenth to the eighteenth century, and even then there is

a difference between Venice or Cracow and Frankfurt am Main. Max Weber's "pariah people?" But how absurd to transfer such untouchable associations to so eminently touchable a people.

So what shall a well-intentioned medievalist do? He shall, forsooth, obtain a grant and wend his way directly to the archives in search of empirical data.

And there, to be sure, he will find abundant rewards. There is hardly a major archive in Europe, be it national, provincial, or municipal, which does not harbor hoards of documents relating to the Jews, most of them unexplored even after more than a century of digging and publishing. Just last summer a young Catalan came from Barcelona to the Fifth World Congress of Jewish Studies in Jerusalem and delivered a stunning paper in impeccable Hebrew. He has found no less than 1,100 documents in the Archivo de la Corona de Aragón relating to the events of *one year*—the anti-Jewish massacres of 1391.

Now I should be the very last to minimize the importance of archival research for the reconstruction of Jewish history. Indeed, would that we possessed comprehensive volumes of archival *regesta* for the Jews of every country in which they lived. But whether or not that will eventually come to pass, it seems clear that we shall be seeing an increasing number of books and monographs in medieval history based almost entirely on archival documents involving Jews. Such subjects are already in growing vogue for dissertations here and in Europe. As the trend broadens, more and more such studies will be presented as "Jewish history," rather than as what they really are—valuable building blocks for the very aspects of Jewish history which they purport to treat.

For what is contained in the archives represents, intrinsically, only a partial view of the Jews. These are materials which derive from their external relations and reflect, so to speak, their "foreign affairs." What they reveal of the Jews is no more comprehensive and balanced than what could be elicited for American history if one had to depend exclusively on materials in the British, French, or German archives.

It is the same with other types of sources to which medievalists turn for enlightenment. To this day the history of Judaeo-Christian polemics generally means the history of what the Christians said against the Jews. If the source be belletristic, it is again the non-Jewish literature which is explored, and the mirror is held, not by the Jews, but the others. There were no neutral or sympathetic gentile observers in the Middle Ages to speak of. Medieval Jewry had no Tocqueville to describe it.

But let us return to the archives.

By and large the documents naturally reflect those aspects of the Jews which were of direct interest to the governing power—crown, papacy, duke, bishop, or municipality. When they looked at the Jews, what did they see?

In the eyes of the government the Jewish community was essentially the tax-gathering agency of the Jews. It was primarily in order to strengthen this central function that all ruling powers, whether in the Christian West or the Muslim East, granted Jewish communities a latitude of corporate autonomy so broad as to be almost inconceivable today. The state was interested in Jewish taxes, and it taxed the Jews collectively. The community was responsible for a bulk sum, and it apportioned and gathered the taxes on its own from its individual members.

Yet upon this seemingly limited and mundane sub-

structure Jews throughout the medieval world maintained a *civilization*, as comprehensive, in its way, as
anything in Christendom or Islam. If they had no single
unified territory, its surrogates were the Jewish quarter
or the Jewish street. If they possessed no sovereign national state, they had it in microcosm in the *kahal*, the
self-governing Jewish community. Using its power of
taxation as a basic instrument of social control, the community built up an elaborate institutional structure. The
synagogue was as much town hall as house of prayer.
Civil and criminal cases (in Spain even capital crimes)
were adjudicated in Jewish courts of law according to
Jewish jurisprudence. The community regulated its own
markets. Brotherhoods busied themselves with the entire gamut of charity and social welfare. Education was
provided in Jewish schools, which ranged from the primary level to the academy. Anchored in a Jewish society which embraced the whole of life, culture could
oscillate between tension and symbiosis with the non-
Jewish environment and yet maintain its inner integrity
and continuity.

Only the jagged outer edges of all this will surface in
the archives. For the rest one can only turn to the Jewish
sources. These are by no means restricted to literary
sources. Though many communal minutebooks (*pink-
asim*) have perished, those that survive are invaluable
to the historian. But it is especially the thousands of
extant medieval rabbinic *responsa* which constitute, in
their ensemble, the greatest Jewish documentary reposi-
tory of all. In the main these are actual legal cases involving individuals of communities which were submit-
ted to eminent rabbinic jurists, who then "responded"
with their decisions. For all practical purposes they may
be termed "Jewish archives." And what a pulsating,
richly variegated world they reveal! There is hardly an

aspect of Jewish public or private life that is not illumined by them in concrete and abundant detail.

In sum, unless one has access to such texts, to say nothing of the staggering range of Hebrew literary sources, one will end up not with Jews but with "archival Jews"—taxpayers, tax-farmers, moneylenders, court-Jews when they are at the royal court, but not when they are at home. We shall perceive, not the normal inner development, but the crisis or the exceptional event—a massacre, a new governmental imposition and Jewish efforts to avert it, a conflict of jurisdiction. Whatever their other sins, it must be said for twentieth-century Judaic scholars that they have by no means neglected the archives or the non-Jewish languages and sources relevant to their fields. Question: How many general medievalists who have spoken of the Jews have ever bothered to familiarize themselves with the Jewish liturgy? With minor regional variations, that liturgy was recited by all medieval Jews, rich and poor, scholars and *vulgus*, whether in Paris or Baghdad, three times each day. Is it not possible that even a cursory acquaintance with the medieval Jewish prayerbook might have some relevance for an understanding of medieval Jewish life and aspirations?

6

However even linguistic competence and knowledge of sources are but a *praeparatio*. What the historian finds is at least determined in part by his fundamental orientation.

What is required?

Perhaps it would be best to proceed, *via negativa*, to consider what is *not* required.

An old Jewish adage exclaims—"Woe to me from mine enemies, and woe to me from my friends." I speak to the friends.

It is not a matter of "Jewish contributions to civilization," though when the entire story is told the Jewish share in medieval civilization may well turn out to be larger than we would even imagine today. But as a primary historiographical motive it must lead in a false direction. Whether Américo Castro is correct in affirming the "primary decisive function of the Hispano-Hebrews" in the history of Spain, whatever one's opinion of the function of the Jews in international trade before the rise of Venice and Genoa, however impressed one may be by the staggering list of translations assembled by Steinschneider in that formidable tome, *Die Hebräische Übersetzungen des Mittelalters*—history thus focused will only pick up the Jews at their points of outside contact and ignore them when they are alone among themselves. Medieval Jews did not awake each day to ponder—"what shall I contribute today?" Nor did they generally conceive of themselves as impressarios of cultural contact, the Sol Huroks of the Middle Ages. Most of what they created, they created for their own needs. If that also passed over and fructified the culture of the nations, so much the better for the nations, and none the worse for the Jews.

It is not a matter of Jewish sources for general history either, though such sources exist in profusion. Professor Goitein's masterful reconstruction of *A Mediterranean Society* out of Genizah fragments is appropriately titled; it retrieves for us all not only a Jewish society, but hitherto lost chapters in the history of the Near East as a whole. In Sofia, of all places, the Historical Institute of the Bulgarian Academy has already published two volumes with the resounding title: *Fontes Hebraici ad*

*Res Oeconomicas Socialesque Terrarum Balcanarum
Pertinentes.* They consist entirely of rabbinic *responsa*
which contain information for Balkan economic and
social history otherwise unavailable, with each text
given in Hebrew and Bulgarian, together with a French
précis. The mine of general historical information in the
responsa emanating from other parts of Europe, from
North Africa and Asia, have so far hardly been touched
by the general historian. In terms of our discussion,
however, these must be characterized as fringe benefits.
They are not the central issue.

Nor is it a matter of "parallels," that peculiar mode
whereby, if at all, lip-service is rendered to Jewish intellectual history in so many textbooks on the Middle
Ages. Christian Europe had its Aquinas, the Jews their
Maimonides, and thus the index at the end of the book
can boast an entry for "Philosophy, Jewish." But the
section on Aquinas usually flows out of an integrated
consideration of the development of Christian philosophy as a whole, and of scholasticism in particular,
whereas Maimonides appears suddenly with no philosophical antecedents, companions, opponents, or prog-
eny.

Two further caveats are in order, I think, because of
the times in which we live and work.

It is not, or should not be, a matter of what I would
call an expiatory *leidensgeschichte* in the wake of the
Nazi Holocaust. Heaven knows, the history of Jewish
suffering in the Middle Ages is real enough and should
be known to the full. The destruction of European Jewry a generation ago was prepared in many ways by a
"teaching of contempt" in the Middle Ages whose own
roots go back even earlier. Professor Ruether will have
more to say about that. Again, if the Holocaust is not
merely a Jewish issue, as it is surely not, but also a har-

rowing symptom of other malignancies deep in the heart of Western civilization, then all the prior evidence must be assembled. And yet—precisely because this task is so compelling—one must beware of reducing medieval Jewish history to a history of antisemitism or a record of pogroms. In so doing, with the best of intentions you also reduce the Jews to passive objects of history rather than active subjects and thus again deny that Jewish history exists. To know the Jews you must inquire as to what they were doing *between* pogroms and ponder not just how they died, but above all, how they *lived*.

Finally, one must also beware today of a seductive anachronism, the casting back into the Middle Ages of one's favorite modern Jewish neoarchetypes. In the intellectual culture of the modern West the Jew looms as both historical prototype and mythic symbol of an alienation which is at least as much a source of pride as of malaise. The Jew as outsider and alien grips the imagination. The myth, fostered by Jewish and gentile intellectuals alike, has become a major motif in some of the best literature of the century. Ahasuerus, the Wandering Jew, has been updated to the point where not only does he no longer repel, he positively attracts us as a kindred spirit.

Be that as it may, one thing should be made clear. Whether or not Leopold Bloom walks the streets of Dublin, and even if Moses Herzog remembers his Yiddish, their problems are not those of their medieval forebears. The alienation of so many modern Jews is dual in nature. Strangers to gentile society even after emancipation, they had lost their Jewish moorings in the struggle to achieve it. The limbo in which they found themselves is a peculiarly modern Jewish phenomenon. At his most alienated from the Christian or Muslim environment, the medieval Jew had at least the security of closeness to his community and his people, and a texture of shared memories, future hopes, and present meaning.

In fact, however, even his proverbial alienation from the gentiles must be understood and qualified in time and place. Medieval Jews by no means always felt themselves strangers in an immediate and personal sense. One of the exiles of 1492 can still speak of Spain as "our mother." A Jew can refer to France as *Eretz hatzevi*, "the lovely land," a Hebrew phrase normally applied only to Palestine itself. Above all medieval Jews certainly saw neither virtue nor glamor in alienation, only an abnormal condition that must one day be terminated. To that end they prayed daily for a speedy redemption and, in every age, erupted in messianic movements.

7

What, then, does medieval Jewish history have to offer in and of itself?

The real question should be addressed, not to Jewish history, but to the historian. It concerns his fundamental seriousness and his willingness to free himself from preconceptions inherited or contemporary. He should decide, once and for all, if his view of the Middle Ages does not remain parochial if it glosses over so ubiquitous a presence as that of the Jews. He must determine whether that which was created on the soil of Europe, Asia, or Africa in the Middle Ages is not part of "history," even when it does not directly affect majority history but develops in its own way and persists on its own terms. And if he affirms that he is indeed obliged to take the Jewish experience into account, he must further answer to himself whether he has fulfilled his function by a few passing remarks which perpetuate the clichés that already abound in the literature.

The rest, and perhaps the gravest aspect, concerns his obligation not merely to his craft, but toward that ultimate illumination of the entire human condition which I assume to be his own deepest *raison-d'être* as historian.

Whatever the pretensions of the Enlightenment or the nineteenth century, it is we who live in the first age in which a truly universal history has not only begun to be possible, but has also begun to filter onto the shelves of the paperback bookstore. If we pursue our difficult and solitary labors on the tacit assumption that the entire human record, whether of ancient Hittites or remote Polynesians, has something to add toward an understanding of Man, then surely medieval Jewish history and civilization claim their place by right and not by sufferance.

Our accelerating contact with other civilizations, and a keen awareness of the impasse of our own, have dented, to say the least, the Western triumphalist reading of history as never before. Just as we no longer feel comfortable in a simplistic equation of ancient civilization with Greece and Rome, or of the modern world with Europe and America, so the way is open for a second look at the Middle Ages as well. This should be done not only with eyes to see the variety of its cultures, but also because a history written merely from the vantage point of power and numbers must increasingly seem shallow to us.

If on a superficial level the history of medieval Jewry is the history of the vanquished, it loses nothing thereby in significance. Quite to the contrary. How men cope with historical catastrophe and suffering, how they can continue to create under conditions that seem otherwise unpropitious, is something we ignore today at our own risk. To be sure, the Jews have not been the only minority in history, nor the only defeated people. But they have been the classical minority everywhere, and, among the defeated, they have left perhaps the most sustained and articulate record. No mean history, this. How such a people was able in the Middle Ages to maintain a worldwide unity without a visible temporal or ecclesiastical hierarchy to enforce it; how it interacted with its many and diverse host-cultures while yet stamping even that which it borrowed with its own seal; how it withstood the victorious taunts of its two daughter religions, living in history while refusing to accept the "verdict" of history—these are surely historical themes as grand as any to be found in the rise and fall of empires and cannot be left to Jewish historians alone.

Ladies and gentlemen, you misread me if you consider this either a rebuke or a plea. It is, rather, a renewal of an open invitation which you have had in hand for a century and a half. So long as you do not respond, we shall continue with our work. We shall miss your contributions. But in the end it is you who will remain impoverished.

THE *ADVERSUS JUDAEOS*
TRADITION IN THE
CHURCH FATHERS:
THE EXEGESIS OF
CHRISTIAN ANTI-JUDAISM

Rosemary Radford Ruether

The primary materials for studying the attitudes towards
the Jews in the Church Fathers are the *Adversus Judaeos* writings.[1] These writings are remarkable for their
preservation of the archaic "testimonies tradition." The
earliest Christian scripture before the written New
Testament was the Jewish Bible, or "Old Testament,"
Christologically interpreted. Along with this Christological interpretation of the "Old Testament" there developed from the beginning an anti-Judaic "left hand."
This anti-Judaic "left hand" of Christological interpretation was designed to show why the Jewish religious
community, from which Christianity got both its Scripture and its messianic hope (which it believed to be
fulfilled in Jesus), did not accept this "fulfillment" of
its own tradition. In effect the Church sought to discredit
the rival rabbinic exegesis of this same Scripture and to
build up a case against the Jewish religious community

and its teachers in order to confirm its own faith as the authentic culmination of the Jewish religious tradition.[2]

Both the Christological and anti-Judaic exegesis of the Old Testament preexisted and formed the hermeneutical basis of the New Testament itself. But this tradition continues and expands in the Church Fathers as a collection of themes and proof-tests designed to prove that Jesus is the Christ predicted by the prophets and that the Jewish community, which rejects this faith, is both blind and reprobate. The Old Testament itself continues to be the basic Scripture for this hermeneutical work, although in the Patristic collections and treatises one or two New Testament references may be added to the Old Testament testimonies. (Even though in this paper I will follow the Christian convention of referring to the Jewish Scriptures as the "Old Testament," I must note at the outset that this very term itself is a Christological and anti-Judaic *midrash* on the Jewish Scriptures.)

The *Adversus Judaeos* writings include simple catalogues of testimonies arranged by theme with a minimum of exposition, such as Cyprian's *Three Books of Testimonies Against the Jews*, the *Contra Judaeos* by the sixth-century Spanish Father, Isidore of Seville, or the *Selected Testimonies from the Old Testament Against the Jews* by Pseudo-Nyssa. They also include treatises on particular themes, such as Novatian's diatribe "On Jewish Meats," or attempts to gather all the themes systematically, such as Tertullian's *Adversus Judaeos* or Justin Martyr's *Dialogue with Trypho*. The anti-Judaic sermon or series of sermons was another favorite form, the most famous of which is the eight sermons against the Jews preached by John Chrysostom in 386–87. The dialogue treatise gave rise to a whole series of imitations, some of which may have actually been written as a result of arranged disputations between Jews and Christians and some of which are literary conventions. In neither case, however, do we get much sense of what the Jewish spokesmen might have said in their own defense. The Jewish protagonist is a straw figure for the Christian apology. The dialogue form can even be elaborated into a liturgical drama.[3] But throughout these writings from the second to the sixth century the arguments themselves remain fairly continuous and fixed. My purpose in this paper will be to provide a systematized summary of the main anti-Judaic themes which appear in these writings and are, therefore, generally accepted as a part of the content of Christian theology. One must remember that this represents the basic hermeneutical tradition of the Church. All theological writing and preaching were based on this Christological interpretation of the Old Testament, and so, although these themes are specifically summarized in this particular genre of writings, they are assumed as the background of and referred to in every teaching that touched on the Jews. Since a cornerstone of Christian faith was that it fulfilled the messianic predictions of the prophets and that the Church was the New Israel replacing the Old, it was difficult to preach or teach anything without referring to this tradition in some way. The *Adversus Judaeos* tradition, then, informed the prevailing way that the Christian community was taught to look at not only the Jews of the New Testament times, but also Jewish history back to Abraham and the Jewish community of its own times. In the fourth century Christianity became the established religion of the Christianized Roman empire. The anti-Judaic doctrines were then translated into a theological-juridical principle for defining the status of Jews vis à vis the Church in Christendom. It is at this point that we find the connection between the patristic exegetical anti-Judaism and anti-semitism as a legal, sociopolitical practice in Christian society.

The anti-Judaic themes typically fall into two major groupings: a) the rejection of the Jews and the election of the gentiles, and b) the inferiority and spiritual ful-fillment of the Jewish law and cult. Included in this is the rationale for the Christian messianic, spiritualizing interpretation of the Jewish Scriptures themselves.

The reprobation of the Jews is based ultimately on the assertion that they rejected Jesus as the Christ. But, as in the New Testament, the Church Fathers project this act of apostasy backward so as to make it the cul-minating and final act of a history that is a trail of crimes and perfidies. This is not a recent forgivable mis-step. The Jews have ever been apostate from God. The rejection and murder of Christ is the foreordained con-clusion of the evil history of a perfidious people. With the death of Christ the Jews are said to have "filled up the measure of their sins."

The basic form of this idea is to see Jewish history as a heritage of rejecting and killing the prophets, of which the rejection and killing of Christ, the final prophet, are the climax. The theme, begun in the New Testament and carried on in the patristic writings, paints a picture of the Jews as a people who never heard the prophets, always rejected the prophetic message and refused to repent, and finally killed the prophets. The Prophets themselves are divorced from the Jewish peo-ple and are made the heritage of the Church. An his-torical view of Scripture as a divinely written book keeps the Church from raising the question of how the pro-phetic books could have been accepted and preserved by that same people who never "heard the prophets."

The list of the crimes of the Jews had been considerably expanded in the Church Fathers, however. The Jews are also idolators, law-breakers, and evil-doers of every kind. Their proclivity for idolatry and vice is presumed to have been picked up during their stay in Egypt. The Mosaic law, with its cultic and dietary commandments, is seen as a curb upon their Egyptian depravity. God restrained their inordinate appetites with dietary laws and gave them a regulated cult to "innoculate" them against even worse idolatry. Eusebius sums up the matter by saying, "Everything that Moses forbade they had previously done without restraint."[4]

Once out in the desert they were unable to shake off the evil habits picked up in Egypt and fell straightway into idolatry. The Golden Calf is cited as a chief case for this mania for idols. It is the paradigm of their rejection of God, which must finally lead to God's rejection of them. Indeed Barnabas believes that God has already abrogated the covenant with the Jews in favor of the future Church at the time of the Golden Calf, a view found also in the Stephen section of the Book of Acts.[5] Some writers also hint that they resisted Moses and even tried to kill him, but this theme is not prominent, perhaps because of the contradictory desire to deprecate the Mosaic tradition as well.[6]

When in the Promised Land the Jews continued to run after idols. Every prophetic text that rebukes the people for rebelliousness, unfaithfulness, and "whoring after foreign gods" can be ransacked to provide proof of what the Jews were like in those times. Since the gentile Church itself had recently come from paganism, this would seem to be a dubious charge. But the Fathers surmount this by a remarkable piece of historical compression whereby the proclivity of the Jews for idols is contrasted with the "faithful gentiles," who have turned from idols to the worship of the true God in the Christian Church. As Tertullian puts it:

> According to the divine Scriptures the people of the Jews quite forsook God and did degrading service to idols and abandoning Divinity, surrendered to images. . . . And, in later times, in which the kings were governing them . . . they did again worship golden kine and groves and enslave themselves to Baal. Whence it is proven that they have ever been guilty of the crime of Idolatry, whereas our lesser or posterior people quit the idols . . . [and] has been converted to the same God, from whom Israel, as we have shown above, departed.[7]

The prophetic texts can also provide proof of a full array of other crimes: blasphemy, rebelliousness, adultery, and general sensuality. This theme of Jewish sensuality can be fused with the ontological dualism of Christian theology that describes the Jew as a man of the outward letter, a carnal, this-worldly man, as contrasted with the Christian, a man who belongs to the age of the Spirit. Ephrem the Syrian especially draws on the language of Hosea to describe the Synagogue as a harlot, cast off by God because she was "wanton between the legs." Jerusalem is equated with Sodom and Gomorrah.[8] John of Damascene says that God gave the Jews the Sabbath as a time-bound observance because of their "grossness and sensuality" and "absolute propensity for material things," as contrasted with the Christian whose worship belongs to the eschatological or eternal day.[9] Ps. 106:37 especially is used to paint an extraordinary picture of the Jews as infanticides, cannibals, and people who sacrifice their children to idols.[10]

The method employed here is to take the prophetic denunciation out of the context and to attribute it, in an absolute manner, to all Jews, then and now.

The purpose of this catalogue of crimes is to demonstrate that their history tends toward and culminates in the final apostasy of the Jews, which is the rejection and death of the Messiah. The nature of the Jews is fixed as one of monstrous evil and rejection of God, logically culminating in the murder of God's Son and justifying God's final rejection of them. God's efforts on their behalf have always been futile. In his forbearance he sends prophets, whom they reject and murder. With the death of Christ the final "evidence is in" that the Jews are not suitable to be God's people. They are then unequivocally rejected for a second people who are the true heirs of the prophets, namely, the gentile Church, which does accept God's Word.

The crime of killing the Messiah is seldom explicitly called "deicide" in the pre-Nicene Fathers, although this is implicit as soon as Jesus is defined as "Son of God" in the metaphysical sense. Most Fathers regard this as the crime of rejection of the final messianic envoy in the line of the martyred prophets. To reject the Christ is to reject the promised salvation and to put oneself beyond the pale of God's designated means of redemption. With the more developed Nicene theology, the character of the crime could be magnified. The Jews are described as enemies of God who commit a cosmic act of treason and *lèse majesté* against the Sovereign of the Universe. Killing Christ is a cosmic regicide. This theme particularly develops after the Constantinian establishment, when Christian theologians begin to identify the emperor with the Vicar of Christ on earth. Chrysostom specifically calls this a sin of "deicide" (*Theoktonian*).[11]

This proof of the Jews' evil nature, developed by reading prophetic denunciations one-sidedly, was presumed to apply to contemporary Jews also. Since no such evidence of infanticide or gross sensuality does, in fact, seem to characterize their communities, the Church Fathers must explain this, either by hints that such things happen secretly or that, even though they are less evil externally than they used to be, they are actually worse spiritually because of their rejection of Christ. Chrysostom especially plays on this dialectic. Formerly they were prone to every vice and lawlessness, but God kept trying to convert them. Now that they are utterly cast off, they insist on strictly observing all the details of the Law. But since God has now abrogated the Law, this is simply a new perversity on their part. When God wanted them to keep the Law, they would not. Now that God has abolished it, they insist on keeping it. Either way they always do whatever God does not want them to do.[12]

The method of proof-testing this history of Jewish evil consists of splitting the right hand from the left hand of the prophetic message, applying the left hand to the Jews and the right hand to the Church. By this method one gains an unrelieved tale of evil-doing, supposedly characteristic of the Jews, who are divorced from the message of forgiveness and future promise which is applied to the Church. The Jewish Scriptures, which actually contain the record of Jewish self-criticism and repentance, are turned into a remorseless denunciation of the Jews, while the Church itself stands triumphant and perfect, having divorced from itself the heritage of prophetic self-criticism. Anti-Judaism and ecclesiastical triumphalism arise as two sides of the same false polarization of the prophetic dialectic of judgment and promise.

Fundamental to this method is the attempt to prove that, even in the Old Testament, there existed, not one, but two people: an evil apostate people, the Jews, and a faithful people, represented by the heroes and prophets, whose lineage is fulfilled in the future Church. The casting off of the Jews and the election of the gentile Church as the true Israel was known and foretold by the prophets themselves. Only the denunciations of the prophets apply to the Jews. The future promises apply to the Church, not to the Jews. There are several images by which this concept of the two peoples is read back into the Jewish Scriptures. The favorite image comes from the motif of patriarchal sibling rivalry. Ishmael and Isaac, Jacob and Esau, Jacob's elder brothers and Joseph, Manasseh and Ephraim foretell the two peoples; the Church claims the authentic lines of Isaac, Jacob, Joseph, and Ephraim, while relegating the cast-off line to the Jews.[19] The favorite test for this is Gen. 25:23: "Two people" are in Rebecca's womb and "the younger shall overcome the elder and the elder shall serve the younger." The younger people are the gentile Church, which overcomes the elder brother, the Jews, while the elder brother is to be in perpetual servitude to the younger people, the Church.[14]

This image of the two brothers can be made more startling by tracing it back to Cain and Abel. God rejected the sacrifices of Cain, i.e. the Jewish sacrificial system, while accepting the spiritual sacrifice of the Church. The exiled and reprobate status of the Jews can be compared with that of Cain.[15] This becomes a typological ancestor for the myth of the Wandering Jew. As the fourth-century poet Prudentius puts it:

From place to place the homeless Jew wanders in ever-shifting exile, since the time when he was torn

> from the abode of his fathers and has been suffer-
> ing the penalty for murder and having stained his
> hands with the blood of Christ, whom he denied,
> paying the price of sin. . . . This noble race (is)
> scattered and enslaved. . . . It is in captivity under
> the younger faith . . . a race that was formerly un-
> faithful confesses Christ and triumphs. But that
> which denied Christ is conquered and subdued and
> has fallen into the hands of Masters who keep the
> Faith.[16]

The image of the two brothers could also draw on the
Pauline exegesis of the two wives, Sarah and Hagar or
Rachel and Leah.[17] Hagar the bondswoman and her
children are cast off. She is the type of the fallen, earthly Jerusalem, which is in bondage together with her
children—bondage both in the sense of political bondage in exile under the nations (the gentile Church!)
and also in the sense of moral bondage to material
things. The Church is the eschatological spiritual Israel,
which has been freed by Christ.[18] Like Leah, the Synagogue is "weak-eyed," blinded by the "veil" of the
Torah, and unable to read the spiritual message of God.
This language could be mingled with that of Hosea,
which likens Israel to a harlot, to typify the Synagogue
as the cast-off harlot in contrast to the Church, the true
bride of Christ. This image of the Church as a triumphant bride in contrast to the Synagogue who stands
with broken staff and rejected air, a blind over her eyes,
was a favorite motif depicted on medieval cathedrals.[19]

The contrast between the old Israel and the Church
is typically assimilated into a contrast between Jews and
gentiles. There is little attempt to retain Paul's concept
of a Jewish remnant into which the Church is ingrafted.
The relation becomes one of straight substitution. This

too was foretold by the prophets. God's promise to Abraham that he would be a father "to many nations" is cited to prove that the true descendants of Abraham are not the Jews, but the nations, i.e., the gentiles.[20] All the texts about Israel as a light to the nations, and about the future sway of the Davidic king over the nations, all praise for non-Hebrew people in contrast to unfaithful Israel, are taken up to prove a promised people who are to be called out from among the gentiles. On the other hand, all the enemies of the prophets and the Davidic king must be read to refer to the Jews. This means, at times, a very selective reading of the Psalmic texts, especially since the enemies which the Davidic king is to conquer and disperse must be read as Jews, while the nations that he is to inherit and rule over must be regarded as the future gentile church! Needless to say, in the original text both the enemies and the nations to be conquered generally refer to outside peoples.[21]

The future promises of the conversion of the gentiles are regarded as proof of the prediction of the gentile Church. This gathering of a faithful people from among the gentiles the Church Fathers (and the New Testament) regard as a fulfillment of the messianic expectation of the ingathering of the "nations" to Zion at the time of redemption. This again requires extraordinary distortion of the original text, for there the Israel which is chastised and the Israel whose messianic fulfillment is predicted are one and the same, while the Church must read the messianic ingathering of the gentiles in an antithetical relation to the chastisement of Israel![22]

After the Constantinian establishment this concept of the universal ingathering of all nations can be identified with the ecumenical empire and the Roman *Pax*. Eusebius especially identifies Christendom with the millennial reign of the Messiah over the earth. Like the Davidic king, the Christian emperior reigns "from sea to sea and from the River to the ends of the earth." All nations gather into this Kingdom of Christ, except the Jews, who alone are in exile "under their enemies." But since their enemies are now the gentile Church, the reversal of Jewish messianic hope becomes total. All nations are redeemed at the coming of Christ except the Jews![23] This blending of messianic fulfillment and Roman universal empire gives the Christian mission to all nations a highly imperialistic character. The mission of the Church becomes one of universal conquest. The success of the Church becomes a proof of divine favor and fulfillment, while the sufferings of the Jews proves their disfavor with God. Needless to say, When Christians are persecuted, the opposite standards are applied, and Christian suffering becomes holy martyrdrom.[24] By the same token the suffering of the Jews is denied any commonality with martyrdom. Chrysostom particularly insists that the "martyrs especially hate the Jews for the reasons that they love so deeply the One who, by them, was crucified," while Jewish suffering is the blameworthy suffering of thieves, grave robbers, and sorcerers.[25]

The climactic theme of the *Adversus Judaeos* tradition is that Jewish reprobation is a permanent and irrevocable condition. The left hand of Christian victory and messianic ingathering of the nations is Jewish exile and servitude "under the nations," now transformed into the New Israel. This exile is to last until the end of time. As evidence of their rejection the Jewish Law has been revoked by God, and they are perverse for continuing to observe it. Their cultic center is destroyed. Temple, priesthood, and sacrificial system have all been terminated. The Jews, therefore, celebrate the festivals illegitimately in the Diaspora. The destruction of the

temple *cultus* signifies the end of the only legitimate
vehicle of worship which God gave to the Jews, indi-
cating that all access to God for them is now cut off.

This view of the destruction of the Temple demands
again a double standard for judging similar developments in the Church and the Synagogue. The noncultic
worship of the Church is regarded as the fulfillment of
that universal spiritual worship among the nations predicted by the prophet Malachi (1:10–11).[26] As the
Church's worship becomes more and more cultic, it is
assimilated into the lineage of the Old Testament priesthood. The Synagogue, in turn, survives the demise of
cultic worship and creates a form of worship centered
in the home and in the assembly for prayer and study.
But this noncultic worship, which likewise is scattered
among all nations, is strictly denied any legitimacy. The
Church uses such texts to prove that its own dispersed
and noncultic worship was predicted by the prophets, as
the divinely ordained successor to the Temple. With a
kind of Sadducean literalism, Christians identified valid
Judaism with the temple cult and Aaronite priesthood,
declaring their fall to be the abrogation of legitimate
Jewish religious existence, while reserving the spiritualizing interpretation of prayer and sacrifice for themselves. The rabbis, on the other hand, interpreted this
same passage in Malachi to refer to the Synagogue,
where the sacrificial cult was superseded by the better
worship of "prayer, thanksgiving, and deeds of loving
kindness."[27]

Chrysostom, who is anxious to erect Christianity into
a new temple *cultus* and sacrificial priesthood, endlessly
vilifies the Synagogue as a place of diabolical worship
and castigates the Jewish community for carrying on the
ancient festivals after the temple cult has fallen. The
permanent destruction of the Temple is the keystone of

his argument that religious Judaism has been abrogated, and its continuation is illegitimate in God's eyes and tantamount to the worship of the devil. Julian the Apostate made a promise to the Jewish community to rebuild the temple. The Christian Fathers erect a myth around this event, claiming that the Jews tried to rebuild the temple three times, but their impious efforts were miraculously beaten back by God each time.[28]

The divinely ordained state of the Jews from Christ until the end of time is that of preservation—but in a state, not of positive divine election, but of negative bondage under divine wrath. The desolation of Jerusalem, the exile of the Jews, and their now inferior status within Christian society are the proofs of divine wrath. The book of Daniel is searched to show that three captivities were predicted. The first two had precise time limits, and the restoration promised the Jews has already been fulfilled in their restoration after the Egyptian and Babylonian captivities. But the third exile has no time limit and is to last until the end of history.[29] The Temple will never be rebuilt. The Jews will never be restored to Jerusalem or the Promised Land. Their exile, dispersion, and bondage under their enemies is their permanent condition until the Second Coming of Christ, when they will have a final chance to repent and acknowledge their error. In vain do the Jews look for a Messiah to deliver them from captivity.

The Church Fathers frequently cite a mistranslated text from Ps. 69:24, "Their back bend thou down always," to characterize this condition of misery that is to be the lot of the Jews in the Christian era. As the second-century Father Hippolytus puts it:

'Let their eyes be darkened that they see not.' And surely ye have been darkened in the eyes of your soul with a darkness utter and everlasting. For now that the true light has arisen, ye wander as in the night and stumble on places with no roads and fall headlong, as having forsaken the way that says, 'I am the Way.' Furthermore hear this yet more serious word: 'And their back do thou bend down always.' That means, in order that they be slaves to the nations, not 430 years, as in Egypt, nor 70 years, as in Babylonia, but bend them to servitude, He says 'always.' How do you indulge vain hopes, expecting to be delivered from the misery that holds you?[30]

Several Church Fathers connect circumcision with this state of reprobation and divine exclusion from return from exile. Circumcision was not given as a mark of divine favor, but with a view to this future status of exile so that the Jews might be recognized and excluded from Jerusalem. Hadrianic law, following the Bar Kochbar revolt, had indeed excluded Jews from reentering Jerusalem. But since other semitic peoples, such as Egyptians, were also circumcized, and since this only applied to men, this link of exclusion from Jerusalem with circumcision is peculiar. Its purpose seems primarily polemical, namely, to reverse the significance of circumcision as a sign of election and to make it instead a mark of Cain, thus fixing the Jew in a state of permanent wandering.[31]

The continued hope of the Jews for the coming of the Messiah especially enrages some Church Fathers. Several hint that Jews actually know that the Messiah has come, since their own Scriptures tell them so. Their pretense of looking for another simply reflects their unwillingness to repent of their evil ways.[32] The Messiah for which they look must be the Devil or the Anti-

Christ. The idea that the Messiah for whom the Jews look is the Anti-Christ was also incorporated into the baptismal ritual for converted Jews in early medieval times.[33] This notion was to continue to reap deadly fruit up to modern times, when the forged *Protocols of the Elders of Zion*, incorporating the idea that the Jews hope and work for a coming reign of the Anti-Christ, came to stand for the entire myth of the International Jewish Conspiracy.[34]

These theories on the election of the gentile Church and the reprobation of the Jews were supplemented by a second cycle of material, which attempted to prove that Christianity supersedes and spiritually fulfills the Law. Christian exegesis deals with the Law and the cult by claiming that the Jewish understanding of these things is unworthy and "carnal," while the Christian possesses the spiritual realization of that which the Jew clings to in a merely outward way. But beyond this there is also the assertion that the Law and cult themselves were intrinsically unworthy and were given by God for a punitive rather than a redemptive purpose. Both of these assertions rest on the claim that the Jewish teachers cannot interpret Scripture. The Jews see only the letter, while the Christians discern the true spiritual meaning.

The Patriarchs obeyed the universal natural Law from the heart. This was a Golden Age of Virtue. The Patriarchs were not Jews, but like the Christians a universal race. Abraham was the father, not just of the Jews, but of "all nations." The universal, spiritual law of Christ is the restoration of this original spiritual religion of patriarchal mankind. The Mosaic law was given only after the Jews fell into abysmal vice during their stay in Egypt. Its purpose was not to lift the Jews to a higher level, but to restore them to that minimal

humanity from the bestiality into which they had fallen.
It was given to restrain vice, not to inculcate virtue. It
was a special, preparatory training for the Jews, who
are worse than the rest of mankind. But it has now been
revoked by God, and the Jews are contumacious to continue to observe it.[35]

But even though the Christians do not keep the Law
outwardly, they are the true law keepers because they
fulfill it inwardly and spiritually. They possess the new
Law of inward obedience promised by Jeremiah. They
possess the circumcision, not of flesh, but of the heart—
the circumcision of repentance.[36] They understand that
the dietary laws refer not to avoidance of particular
animals, for how could animals, who are all a part of
God's creation, be unclean? The real meaning of these
laws is an allegory. They refer to the various brutish
habits which we are to avoid.[37] (This allegorical interpretation of dietary laws was a favorite apologia in
hellenistic Judaism, which Christianity has taken over in
an anti-Judaic manner.[38]) Christians observe not the external Sabbath, which belongs to temporal creation, but
the eschatological Sabbath of the New Creation.[39]

So, too, the cult was given to cure the Jews of the
abominable idolatry into which they had fallen. God
knew that they could only be restrained from their lust
for idols by giving them a regulated cult of their own.
But this cult was limited to Jerusalem, so it could not be
spread to other peoples. And now that it is abrogated,
Judaism has been definitively terminated.[40] It is Christianity which spiritually fulfills the cult, not in the sacrifice of bulls and rams, but in the spiritual sacrifice of
the contrite heart, a spiritual temple which can be spread
to all peoples. Judaism, as we have seen, made a similar
claim for the Synagogue as the spiritual successor to the
Temple.

This concept of supersession and spiritual fulfillment of the law and the cult is based on the dualism between the temporal and the eschatological, which is fundamental to the theology of Paul, to the Epistle to the Hebrews, and to the theology of the Gospel of John.

But in New Testament theology this concept is based on the belief that Christianity represents the eschatological Israel in the sense that it is the beginning of the age of redemption that will soon bring this present era of temporal history to an end. In the Church Fathers, however, this dualism between the historical and the eschatological eras has been historicized so that it becomes a dualism between the old era of unredeemed man, typified by Judaism, and the new historical era of the Church. One draws a line across history at the time of Jesus, which is treated as though it coincides with a transition from sin to grace, from an earlier era of outwardness, carnality, and unbelief, to a new era of inwardness, spirituality, and faith. The Jews receive the negative side of all these dualisms. The Jews are the men of the letter, vis à vis Christian spiritual hermeneutic. The Jews are the carnal men confined in their moral lives to a carnal level of existence, vis à vis Christians, who live on a higher plane, morally and ontologically. Jews are blind vis à vis Christian belief. But this moral and ontological dualism is also treated as though it were a temporal or historical sequence, so that everything Jewish becomes obsolete and has no further right to exist now that its spiritual fulfillment in Christ has come. The earlier revelation only predicts and symbolizes outwardly that which has now been fulfilled inwardly. It has become obsolete, now that its spiritual realization has taken place. As St. Augustine puts it, the Jews "have remained stationary in useless antiquity."[41]

Like the similar dualism between judgment and promise that assigns judgment to the Jews and promise to the Church, this dualism of letter and spirit, as Jewish and Christian eras and forms of humanity, has been a fatal flaw in Christian theology. Judaism is programmatically denied any dimension of inwardness and spirituality. Jews are made morally inferior and historically obsolete. Cultural obliteration of ongoing Jewish history is programmed into Christianity. This still characterizes Christian education and its secular derivatives. But Christianity, in turn, becomes docetic and is unable to deal realistically with its own bodily and historical existence. The constant splintering of Christianity into perfectionist sects is one side of the Christian inability to deal with its own finitude. On the other side there is the institutional triumphalism of Catholic Christianity, which constantly covers up the actual faults of the Church with a theory of spiritual perfection and infallibility that remains invisible to the outward eye.

This anti-Judaic tradition grew into a fixed standpoint between the second and fourth centuries and was to remain the hermeneutical tradition for identifying the Jews in Christian theology in every sermon, biblical exegesis, and theological treatise down through and including Martin Luther's diatribe on the "Jews and their Lies." In the fourth century the Church was transformed from a persecuted sect into the established religion of the Christianized empire. With this change the anti-Judaic tradition ceased to be a private battle between Church and Synagogue and became the basis of a new legal and social view of the Jews expressed in law and custom. Within the framework of what now was official social policy, the Church decreed misery and cultural obliteration of the Jew, but not physical extermination. Indeed the ambivalence of Christian theology toward the Jew is that it demanded, simultaneously, the ongoing preservation of the Jews, but only in a status of reprobation, clearly visible by their external social oppression, serving as a continuing witness to the divine favor of the Church and as an ultimate witness to the coming of Christ at the end of time. It was from this contradiction that the tragic history of the Jews in Christian society was to descend to increasingly worsening levels of jealous concern and paranoid projection.

Today it is incumbent upon the Christian Church to take responsibility for this history and to acknowledge clearly its own responsibility for creating and fostering it. This has been done so far only superficially. The Christian Church has been willing to prune back the wilder growths of antisemitic rhetoric, but it has been unwilling to deal with the roots of this growth in its own theological structures of faith in Jesus as the Christ whom the Jews "rejected." The Christian Church must do this to become honest about its own history and to attempt very belatedly to rectify its relation to the Jewish community. But just as much it must do this in order to correct a fatal flaw in its own theological structures. In other words, anti-Judaism, unlike Jewish self-defense against Christianity, is not just an external problem of relations with another community, but an internal problem of its own understanding of its faith. The theology of messianic fulfillment, once and for all, 2000 years ago created a world view peculiarly fraught with internal suppressions of reality and external projections of the unredeemed side of existence upon others, archetypally the Jews. Body and Spirit, works and faith, outward letter and inward meaning, Judgment and Promise, particularism and universalism, sinful and gracious existence: all these dualisms, which must properly be understood dialectically, were split into Christian and

Judaic opposites. The unredeemed side of every dualism is projected upon the Jews, the triumphalistic self-righteous side on Christianity. This tendency to paranoia and perfectionism in Christian theology is the internal flaw that has continually marred Christianity's ability to speak the gospel as a message of truthful self-understanding. To correct this flaw we must go back to the root and reexamine Christology itself, that is to say, that theology of fulfilled messianism which continually impedes our ability to speak truthfully about our own ongoing, unredeemed existence in an unredeemed world.

NOTES

1. Rosemary Ruether, *Faith and Fratricide: The Christian Theological Roots of Anti-Semitism* (New York, 1974).
2. I. Rendel Harris, *Testimonies*, I,II (Cambridge, 1961).
3. Arthur Lukyn Williams, *Adversus Judaeos* (Cambridge, 1935).
4. Eusebius, *Demonstrations of the Gospel* I, 16,17.
5. Epistle of Barnabas 4:8; Acts 7.
6. John Chrysostom, *Orations Against the Jews* 6,2; Origen, *Contra Celsus* II, 75.
7. Tertullian, *Adversus Judaeos* in *Ante-Nicene Fathers* III (New York, 1926) ed. A. Cleveland Coxe, pp. 151–52.
8. Ephrem, *Rhythm Against the Jews* 12.
9. John Damascene, *On the Orthodox Faith* IV, 23 ("On the Sabbath").
10. John Chrysostom, *Orations Against the Jews* 6,2 and 5,6.

11. *Ibid.*, 1,7.
12. *Ibid.*, 4,2 and 6,6-7.
13. Maximinius, *Treatise Against the Jews* 1.
14. Cyprian, *Three Books of Testimonies Against the Jews* I,19,21; *Epistle of Barnabas*, 13:2-4; Tertullian, *Against the Jews* 1; Irenaeus, *Against the Heresies* 4,21,2; Augustine, *Against the Jews* 7(9), etc.
15. Aphrahat, *Demonstrations Against the Jews* 16,8; Ephrem, *Rhythm Against the Jews* 8.
16. Prudentius, *Apotheosis* 11. 541-50, ed. and tr. H. J. Thomson (Cambridge, Mass, 1949-53).
17. Gal. 4:21-31; Rom. 9:13.
18. Augustine, *Against the Jews* 5 (6); Cyprian, *Testimonies* I,20.
19. Wolfgang S. Seiferth, *Synagogue and Church in the Middle Ages: Two Symbols in Arts and Literature* (New York, 1970).
20. Rom. 4:11; Epistle of Barnabas 13:7; Justin, *Dialogue with Trypho* 119.
21. Tertullian, *Against the Jews* 12,13.
22. Ephrem, *Rhythm Against the Jews* 20.
23. Eusebius, *Oration on Constantine* 16, 4-8; Chrysostom, *Demonstration to the Jews and Gentiles that Christ is God*.
24. Aphrahat, *Demonstrations Against the Jews* 21.
25. John Chrysostom, *Orations Against the Jews* 6,2.
26. Justin Martyr, *Dialogue with Trypho* 117; Tertullian, *Against the Jews* 5; Augustine, *Against the Jews* 9(12).
27. Jacob Neusner, *Aphrahat and Judaism* (Leiden, 1971), p. 174.
28. Chrysostom, *Orations Against the Jews* 5,10-11.
29. Lactantius, *Divine Institutes* 4,11,18; Hippolytus,

Expository Treatise Against the Jews 6; Aphrahat, *Demonstrations Against the Jews* 19; John Chrysostom, *Orations Against the Jews* 5,1,5; 6,12, etc.

30. The same passage appears often in Augustine; cf. *Against the Jews* 5(6), and 7(10); *City of God* 17,19 and 18,46. The Hebrew text is difficult to understand.

31. Justin Martyr, *Dialogue with Trypho* 16; Tertullian, *Against the Jews* 3; Irenaeus, *Against the Heresies* 2,16,1.

32. Hippolytus, *Refutation of all Heresies* 9,25; John Chrysostom, *Orations Against the Jews* 5,9–10; Augustine, *Against the Jews* 18(34); Eusebius, *Demonstrations of the Gospel* 8,2.

33. James Parkes, *The Jew in the Medieval World* (London, 1938), pp. 304,394–400.

34. Norman Cohn, *Warrant for Genocide: The Myth of the Jewish World Conspiracy and the Protocols of the Elders of Zion* (New York, 1966).

35. Eusebius, *Demonstrations of the Gospel* 1,2,16–17; Tertullian, *Against the Jews* 2; Novatian, *On Jewish Meats* 3.

36. Deut. 10:16; Jer. 4:4; 9,26; Rom. 2:25,29; Gal. 5, etc. Epistle of Barnabas 9:1–5; Justin Martyr, *Dialogue with Trypho* 24; Tertullian, *Against the Jews* 3; Cyprian, *Testimonies* 1,8; John Chrysostom, *Orations Against the Jews* 2,1; Isidore of Seville, *Against the Jews* 2,16.

37. Novatian, *On Jewish Meats* 3; Justin Martyr, *Dialogue with Trypho* 20.

38. Aristeas, 128–170; Philo, *De Specialibus Legibus* 4,106–8; *Agr.* 145.

39. John Damascene, *On the Orthodox Faith* 4,23; Epistle of Barnabas 15:8–9; Justin Martyr, *Dia-*

logue with Trypho 21; Tertullian, *Against the Jews* 4; Augustine, *Against the Jews* 2; Aphrahat, *Demonstrations Against the Jews* 13,13.

40. Chrysostom, *Orations Against the Jews* 4,7.
41. Augustine, *Against the Jews* 6(8).

ASPECTS OF JEWISH LIFE

IN ISLAMIC SPAIN

Norman A. Stillman

My heart's in the East
While I'm in the furthermost West.
How can I taste what I eat?
And how can it please?
—Judah ha-Levi

The yearning for Zion was nothing at all unique in medieval Hebrew poetry, even among the highly urbane and assimilated Jews of al-Andalus, or Islamic Spain. The all-powerful Samuel ha-Nagid Ibn Naghrēla (d. 1056), vizier of the Zirid kings of Granada, expressed his longing for the Temple Mount and his desire to serve as a Levite before the altar of the Lord.[1] Yet when Judah ha-Levi, the poet laureate of Andalusian Jewry, began to take these verses seriously and suddenly in the twilight of his years totally rejected his society and its outlook on life, people were stunned. His nationalistic treatise *The Kuzari*, glorifying rabbinic Judaism and rejecting philosophy, was a scandal. But it has always been the fate of Cassandras and Jeremiahs not to be heeded. Approximately thirty years after Judah ha-Levi's renunciation of the joys of Sefarad, the Almohads, a Berber nationalist and fanatically sectarian movement which came out of the mountain fastness of the Ante-Atlas in Morocco, put an end to the Jewish presence in Muslim Spain.[2] A century after that the Inquisition began to make itself felt in Christian Spain, where Andalusian Jewry had reestablished itself, although it would be two hundred years before the *coup de grâce*.

I should like, however, to direct my attention to the society upon which Judah ha-Levi had so dramatically turned his back. It has become commonplace to refer to the "Golden Age of Spain," and so indeed it seemed to the nineteenth-century German Jewish historians like Heinrich Graetz, Leopold Zunz, or Moritz Steinschneider, when they compared it with the European experience. Though our own view may be somewhat more subdued, nonetheless, the period comprising the tenth through twelfth centuries was unique and not without glory. Even if we were to decide that this epoch had been only a Silver Age, we could not deny its luster.

HISTORICAL SKETCH

The Jewish presence in Spain is of great antiquity, perhaps going back as far as Punic times (cf. Jonah 1:3. "But Jonah rose up to flee unto Tarshish from the presence of the Lord").[3] The oldest archaeological evidence dates from the Roman period. In the sixth century we find the Jews an important and formidable element in Visigothic *Hispania*. They were the very core of whatever remained of the middle classes and provided necessary mercantile services as *negotiatores*, including *transmarini negotiatores*.[4] Yet on the eve of the Muslim invasion in 711, we find the Jews a bitterly disaffected element in the society because of the on-again-off-again persecutions by the Visigothic and ecclesiastical authorities that culminated in the harsh decrees of the Sixteenth Council of Toledo in 693, which virtually barred them from carrying on trade, and a year later by the Seventeenth Council of Toledo, which totally disenfranchised those who did not accept baptism. Their thorough disaffection was probably little mitigated by the fact that the subsequent monarch, Witiza (702–710), did not attempt to implement the decrees fully.[5]

Thus as in the case of the Byzantine East, we find the Jews looking to the Muslim invaders as liberators sent by Divine Providence.[6] This parallel to Middle Eastern Jewry's reception of the Muslim armies is, however, superficial. There are some substantial qualitative differences. The Iberian Jews apparently maintained close ties with their brethren across the narrow Straits of Gibraltar. Indeed they were accused at the Seventeenth Council of Toledo of conspiring with their North African coreligionists to hand over Spain to the Muslims. This charge may have had some truth to it in view of the Jews' desperate situation—although it does assume a great deal.[7] The widespread Jewish collaboration with the Muslim troops invading Spain seems almost unique in the history of the Islamic conquests.[8] The only comparable example in the Middle East is the report in al-Balādhurī of an individual Jew aiding the Arabs in the conquest of Caesarea.[9] In Spain, on the other hand, in city after city Ṭāriq and his lieutenant Mughīth organized the local Jews into militia garrisons to stand guard in their absence. We should remember that the first Muslim invasion force was almost totally Berber, not Arab, their number relatively small, and that they were far more overextended than had been the case in the earlier conquests.

During the first century of Islamic rule in Spain the Jews seem to have maintained a relatively low profile —and for good reasons. They had no place in the often sanguinary internal Muslim dissensions, such as the Qays-Yemen enmity or the Arab-Berber disputes. Furthermore, during the later years of the Umayyad Caliphate of Damascus the crystalization of discriminatory laws for *dhimmīs*—as members of the tolerated monotheistic faiths are called in Islam—added a restrictive element.[10]

Arabic sources are notably silent about the Jews during the early years of the Umayyad emirate in Spain. This silence is in part due to the fact that Arab historians were more concerned with the constant wars with the Christian North. It probably also reflects the fact that the Jews were a well-assimilated minority, whose loyalty was not questioned. That Jews moved about rather freely and were unimpeded in their intercourse with the rest of the populace is indicated by a letter from Pope Hadrian I, sent in 785 to the Spanish bishops. In it he requests that they take action to prevent Jewish influence on their flock.[11]

It appears that the Jewish community of Spain felt confident enough at this time to engage in proselytizing activities amongst the Christian population. To do so among the Muslims would have been, of course, unthinkable, since both apostasy and the invitation to apostasy are crimes punishable by death. (It should be noted, however, that under strict Muslim law conversions within the Dār al-Islām can only be made to the dominant faith.)[12] The end of the eighth century witnessed a rash of Christian heresies in northern Spain, some of which manifested Judaizing tendencies.[13] These were followed by the appearance of the proselyte Bodo-Eleazar, formerly a deacon at the court of Louis the Pious. After his conversion to Judaism in 838 in Saragossa, Bodo-Eleazar waged an open campaign against Christianity and engaged in a literary polemic with the Christian nationalist Alvaro.[14] Even if the Christian allegations that he served in the Muslim armed forces and incited the Muslim authorities into giving the Christians the unlikely choice of converting to Islam or Judaism is only apocryphal,[15] it is still indicative of the fact that the Jews of Spain were a force to be reckoned with.

W. Montgomery Watt is not quite accurate in stating that during this period "the Jews stood somewhat apart from the general life of the country, though they came to have a share in its intellectual life."[16] They simply seem to have had no part in the various uprisings, such as that of the *muwallad* Ibn Ḥafsūn, nor did they present any difficulties to the Muslim authorities, as did some Christians in ninth-century Cordova who, under the influence of Spera-in-Deo and his disciples Eulogius and Alvaro, sought out martyrdom by publicly denouncing the Prophet Muḥammad and his faith.[17] The Jews are so rarely mentioned in the Muslim sources for this period because they were so well-assimilated. Even notable Jewish figures such as the vizier Abū Saʿd al-Tustarī, who was prominent at the Fatimid court between 1036 and 1047, merit only a few lines in the histories of the period.[18] Though there do not seem to have been Jews of such prominence in ninth-century Spain, there were those who moved in court circles in Cordova. According to al-Maqqarī, the great compiler of Andalusian cultural history, a Jew by the name of Abu ʾl-Naṣr Manṣūr was court musician to the emir al-Ḥakam I (796–822); it was through Abu ʾl-Naṣr's efforts that the famous Persian singer Ziryāb was brought to Cordova, where—as is well known—he became the undisputed arbiter dictum of social canons and tastes at the court of ʿAbd al-Raḥmān II (822–852).[19]

Islamic Spain at the dawn of the ninth century must have had a very large Jewish population whose ranks were continually swelled by immigration from the Levant and North Africa.[20] Despite its size the Jewish community of Islamic Spain was not known for its scholarship. The spread of Talmudic Judaism out of Babylon was not an instantaneous process, but extended over a long period of time. Eliyahu Ashtor is less than cautious in assuming that Spanish Jewry was under talmudic authority shortly after the Muslim conquest.[21] From the Epistle of R. Sherira Gaon (written ca. 992), and especially from Judah b. Barzillay of Barcelona (fl. eleventh-twelfth centuries), we learn that the deposed exilarch Naṭronay b. Ḥabībay, who arrived in Spain about 772, introduced the teaching of the Babylonian Talmud.[22] He did not transform Spain into a center of scholarship, but he did bring it into the orbit of normative rabbinic Judaism under the authority of the Yeshivot in Iraq. This gradual process of rabbinization is further corroborated by the fact that R. ʿAmram Gaon edited his *Sēder*, or "Order of Prayers," at the request of the Spanish Jewish community sometime around 850.[23] The purpose of this prayerbook was not to abolish local Spanish rites and customs, but rather to serve as a guide for communal leaders to keep their service within halakhic bounds. Indeed it was the halakhic portions which were most important to the Spaniards who were not fully versed in Jewish law.

In many respects Jewish scholarly dependence on the East at this time had its parallel in the Muslim community. The Islamic West—and here I include

North Africa as well—was nourished by the East not
only in its religious scholarship, but in its humanistic
and cultural aspects as well. The glorious flowering of
Andalusian *belles lettres* in the eleventh century which
developed refreshing new forms in Arabic poetry (most
notably the *muwashshaḥ*) drew upon a previous century
devoted entirely to the study of Eastern literature. A
very telling anecdote on the cultural situation in Spain
during these formative centuries relates the keen dis-
appointment of the Buwayhid vizier, the Ṣāḥib Ibn
ʿAbbād (d. 995), in reading the *ʿIqd al-Farid* (*The
Unique Necklace*) of the Spanish poet Ibd ʿAbd Rabbih
(d. 940). The Ṣāḥib had expected to find the cream of
Spanish poetry, but with the exception of Ibn ʿAbd
Rabbih's own verses, he found only eastern material in
the anthology.[24]

The period of Andalusian assertion and self-realiza-
tion begins with the declaration of an independent
caliphate by ʿAbd al-Raḥmān III in 929 and flowers
under his successor al-Ḥakam II (961–976). It is precisely at this time that we see the sudden development
of a flourishing, creative, and highly independent
Spanish Jewry.

This sudden efflorescence of Andalusian Jewry was
in no small measure linked to the rise of a remarkable
physician, diplomat, and statesman, Ḥasday b.
Shaprūṭ (905–975), at the court of ʿAbd al-Raḥmān
III and al-Ḥakam II in Cordova. Although he was a
trusted adviser to these two caliphs and at times han-
dled delicate diplomatic negotiations with the Christian kingdoms of the North and with Byzantium,
Ḥasday never apparently sought any official office
higher than that of a supervisor of customs (a role not
infrequently filled by *dhimmī*s in the East as well). He
was content merely to remain a member of the caliphal

medical staff (*dīwān al-aṭibbā'*). This unusual modesty
—or discretion—was almost unique as far as court
Jews in Spain were concerned. In almost every other
respect, however, he set the pattern to be followed by
later Jewish courtiers.

First, he was a man of culture, part of that international fellowship of men of science which typified
the Hellenistic renascence in medieval Islam and
which S. D. Goitein has dubbed the "Intermediate
Civilization."[25] As a physician Ḥasday was doubtless
schooled in the Greek syllabus, which included philosophy, mathematics, and the natural sciences. Thus he
is mentioned in the works of Muslim writers such as
the biographer of the physicians, Ibn Abī Uṣaybiʿa.[26]
At the request of the caliph ʿAbd al-Raḥmān III
Ḥasday undertook the task of making a new, improved
translation of Dioscorides' *De Materia Medica* from a
Greek manuscript sent by the Byzantine emperor. On
the basis of this he became the first physician in Spain
to recreate the legendary compound *theriac* (*tariyāq
al-fārūq*).[27]

Because of his position as the leading Jewish courtier, Ḥasday acted as the secular head of the Spanish
Jewish community. According to the Jewish sources
he bore the Hebrew title of *Nāsī'* (although no Davidic
lineage was implied as in the Middle East).[28] As was
customary for a courtier or man of rank (wealth in such
cases is a corollary), Ḥasday was a patron of the arts
and sciences. As the leading Jew of al-Andalus, he
naturally felt it his duty to be maecenas to his own
brethren. His secretary, Menaḥem b. Sarrūq, poet and
philologist, was the author of the first Hebrew-Hebrew
dictionary (*Sēfer Pitrōnīm*) which, despite its faulty root
system, enjoyed great popularity among the Jews of
France and Germany who could not use Hebrew-

Arabic dictionaries.[29] Under Ḥasday's patronage the North African-born poet Dūnash b. Labrāṭ, Menaḥem's rival, pioneered in the writing of Hebrew poetry employing Arabic metrics. Indeed Dūnash's adaptation of Arabic metrical schemes set the trend which was to become standard for Hebrew prosody in medieval Spain.[30] This innovation was, to be sure, just the beginning of what was to be the greatest flowering in Hebrew literary history since biblical times. "In the days of the Nasi Ḥasday they [the poets] began to chirp, while in the days of Samuel ha-Nagid, they burst into song," writes the twelfth-century historian and apologist Ibn Daud.[31]

Ḥasday's tenure as leader of the Spanish community also marks a turning point in religious life. Jewish tradition attributes this change to the fortuitous arrival of the Italian scholar R. Moses b. Ḥanokh in 972 as the prisoner of Spanish pirates. He was subsequently redeemed and ultimately came to be recognized as chief scholar in Cordova. The story has been deliberately cloaked in romance by Ibn Daud for reasons that have been discussed at length by Gerson Cohen.[32] Furthermore, according to Ibn Daud, with the recognition of R. Moses b. Ḥanokh as chief scholar (a position comparable to that of a grand mufti in later Islam) and his establishment of an academy in Cordova, the Spanish Jews made a complete break with the Babylonian Yeshivot, which were still the chief diocesan authorities for the majority of Jews in the Islamic world.

Cohen tries to play down the significance of the event and, indeed, questions Ibn Daud's statement that the Jews of Spain now directed all their queries to R. Moses b. Ḥanokh and no longer sought *responsa* from the Babylonian *geonim*.[33] Cohen feels that Ibn

Daud's report must be understood "in the light of his [Ibn Daud's] tendency to regard the period of Ḥisdai ibn Shaprut as the dawn of a new era."[34] However Cohen fails to take into account several important factors, first and foremost of which is the character of Ḥasday himself. His extensive correspondence with foreign Jewish communities, his attempts to contact the king of the Khazars, his patronage of Jewish artists and men of letters, some of whom—like Dūnash— were attracted from abroad, his ceaseless efforts to bring in Hebrew books from abroad, all indicate that Ḥasday envisioned Spain as a leading seat of world Jewry. The elevation of R. Moses b. Ḥanokh and the concomitant independence from Babylon were clearly part and parcel of Ḥasday's program. The testimony of the eleventh-century Muslim writer Ṣāʿid al-Andalusī confirms this:

> Ḥasday specialized in the art of medicine and had an exemplary knowledge of the science of Jewish law. He was the first to open for Andalusian Jewry the gates of their science of jurisprudence, chronology, and other subjects. Previously, they had recourse to the Jews of Baghdad in order to learn the law of their faith and in order to adjust the calendar and determine the dates of their holidays. . . . When Ḥasday became attached to al-Ḥakam, gaining his highest regard for his professional ability, his great talent, and his culture, he was able to procure through him, i.e., al-Ḥakam, the works of the Jews in the East which he desired and then taught the Jews of Spain that of which they had been previously ignorant. They were able as a result of this to dispense with the inconvenience which had burdened them.[35]

Ṣāʿid al-Andalusī does not even mention R. Moses b. Ḥanokh. It is Ḥasday who is responsible for the independent course taken by the Jews of Spain. There can be no doubt that a break with the Babylonian authorities ensued. For there is the additional testimony of a Geniza letter from Hai Gaon to R. Jacob b. Nissīm in Qayrawan in which Hai complains that R. Ḥanokh b. Moses, the son and successor of R. Moses b. Ḥanokh, had ignored the correspondence sent to him by Hai's father, Sherira Gaon.[36]

But why this breach with the Yeshivot? Salo Baron has pointed to political elements in the decentralization and disintegration of the world-wide Jewish authority.[37] There was in addition to the political aspect an exclusivist tendency manifest in the Iberian Peninsula—not only among the Sefardic Jews and not only during the Islamic period, but throughout the course of Spanish history. Another factor which must be kept in mind was the growth of a great spiritual and intellectual center of Jewry in Qayrawan, which at that time was the capital of Tunisia.[38] Qayrawan was the rival of Cordova in the Muslim West politically and culturally throughout the ninth and tenth centuries under the Aghlabids, the Fatimids, and the Zirids. This rivalry could not help but be carried over into the Jewish community as well. Unlike the Cordovans, the Qayrawanese Jews did not embark on an independent course, but maintained the very closest of ties with the Yeshivot into the middle of the eleventh century.[39] This strong bond between Qayrawan and the Yeshivot was maintained despite the fact that the Fatimids and their successors, the Zirids, were totally inimical to the Baghdad caliphate, which tends to negate Baron's contention that Muslim rulers encouraged separatist tendencies in the local Jewish communities.[40] Spanish exclusivism derived from its isolated position at the western extremity of the Dār al-Islām on the very doorstep of Christian Europe. We must bear this salient geographical fact in mind in order to understand properly the individuality of Andalusian culture.

ANDALUSIAN JEWISH SOCIETY

As we have seen, Andalusian Jewish culture began to flower during the heyday of the caliphate of Cordova. It was to bear full fruit, however, only after the disintegration of unified Muslim authority. The period of the so-called "Party Kings" (Sp. *los reyes de taifas*; Ar. *mulūk al-ṭawā'if*) was not without parallel to Renaissance Italy. In both cases we see a patchwork of bickering petty principalities. In both cases, too, we see men of diverse and extraordinary talents drawn into the service of local rulers. Each court tried to the best of its abilities and resources to recreate in miniature the brilliance of the Umayyads of Cordova. In both Arabic and Hebrew *belles lettres* the competition and rivalry provided a healthy stimulation.[41]

The poetry of the eleventh and early twelfth century is a rather faithful mirror of the ambience of the upper strata of society. Much of it is refined, sensual, and unabashedly hedonistic. When I read it, I cannot help but be reminded of Goitein's delightful description of the biblical Book of Esther, *viz.*, "There is the smell of the wine party in it, pungent and stimulating."[42]

> Hasten to the house of your friend and his wine
> A cup will go round like the sun at his right hand

Claret, the glass purifies it, till pearls are shamed
    by its lustre
The cup sees its beauty and hides it as long as it
    can.
Let it come to me and dispel my cares!
This is the sign of the covenant between us.
All kinds of singers and musicians surround me
Each one with his own individual beauty.
                            —(Judah ha-Levi)

Hebrew love poetry reflects a thorough assimilation
into the sophisticated Islamic milieu. The poet sings
of beautiful young maids and comely young men.
Nehemia Allony may protest and deplore Jefim Schirmann's tasteful and erudite treatment of literary
homosexuality "The Ephebe in Medieval Hebrew
Poetry," but he cannot convincingly gainsay Schirmann's analysis.[43] It is only natural that in a society
which idealized the beardless youth as the paragon of
physical perfection, whom the mystic might contemplate in order to induce the rapture of the Divine
Beauty, homosexuality should appear as a literary
motif. It is also natural that the rather limited social
mobility of women and the sophisticated, secular
ambience of the upper echelons of society would often
allow the prevailing mores to take precedence over the
biblical prohibition. Thus we may reasonably assume
that bisexual tendencies were the norm in the Jewish
upper classes, as among their Muslim neighbors. It is
interesting to note that homosexuality was also present
in Jewish society in the medieval Muslim East, but
was apparently not as common—if the scanty references in the Cairo Geniza documents are any indication.[44]

Medieval Spanish Hebrew poetry also gives us in rather graphic terms an insight into the upper class self-image. The panegyric, for example, was a well-developed genre, since most poets were writing for patrons. To some modern tastes many of these poems seem fawning and servile. The poet seems at first glance to be feeding his maecenas' overinflated ego in order to fill his own purse. There is, of course, much truth in this judgment, but it does not take into account equally hyperbolic encomia written by one great man in honor of another. In traditional Middle Eastern culture, social rank, and distinction were—and in many cases still are—considered to be ordained by God. One's station should be properly recognized and not glossed over. Men in authority deserve particular honor since they reflect in this mundane world the ultimate Divine Authority. A talmudic maxim states that "even the most insignificant of the insignificant, once he is appointed to a position of public authority, is to be regarded as the noblest of the noble." [45] It is in light of this attitude that we must understand the many biblical allusions with their royal and even eschatological associations which pervade these poems. Whether or not these poems and their metaphors represent—as Gerson Cohen has suggested —a surrogate form of messianism in which eschatological yearnings were subliminated into a political program, I am not as yet convinced. [46] The thought is tempting, but one should not give in to temptation too readily. Equally grandiloquent poems were recited in honor of Jewish notables in the East. [47] The greatest poet since the rise of Islam, al-Mutanabbī, was not above making koranic allusions to faculties normally attributed to God in praising his patron, Sayf al-Dawla. [48] The Andalusian Muslim poet al-Munfatil could even go so far as to suggest in his panegyric for the Jewish vizier Samuel ha-Nagid that Muslims should kiss his hands as they would the black stone of the Ka ʿba![49]

It is clear that the upper class of Andalusian Jewry did not suffer from false humility. These grandees exhibited a definite sense of elitism—not only vis à vis their fellow Jews in Spain, but vis à vis their coreligionists abroad. The reason for the superiority of Hebrew *belles lettres* in Spain over all the rest of the Diaspora, according to Moses b. Ezra (d. after 1135), is that the Andalusian Jews were none other than the descendants of the people of Jerusalem who surpassed all other Israelites "in the purity of language and the tradition of legal science."[50] The importance of this linguistic pride cannot be overemphasized. Since the rise of Islam, the Arabs had considered their poetry and their rhetoric to be their greatest cultural heritage. This idea was so ingrained in medieval Islamic society that even a Jew like Moses b. Ezra could write that "because the Arab tribes excelled in their eloquence and rhetoric they were able to extend their dominion over many languages and to overcome many nations, forcing them to accept their suzerainty."[51] Thus the flowering of Hebrew poetry in Spain must be understood as an emphatic assertion of the Jewish secular or national culture's equality with the Arabic. The poet and translator Judah al-Ḥarīzī (d. ca. 1235) states quite candidly that he composed his *Taḥkemōnī*, which is patterned after the highly esteemed *Maqāmāt* of al-Ḥarīrī, in order "to show the power of the Holy Language to the Holy People."[52]

This self-conscious pride, which was concerned with purity of lineage, language, and religious tradition, is a hallmark of Hispano-Arabic society. It was to become a still more dominant factor in later Spanish history.[53] As a frontier region Spain showed a marked preference for "that old-time religion." The tenth-century geographer al-Muqaddasī reports that the Spanish Muslims are Mālikīs and recognize only the Koran and the *Muwaṭṭa'* (the record of Mālik's teachings). He goes on to say that "if they learn of any Ḥanafī or Shāfiʿī, they expel him, and if they detect any Muʿtazilite or Shīʿite or the like, they often kill them."[54] This report is, to say the least, a gross exaggeration. It reflects, nonetheless, a psychological truth, for this was how the Spaniards wished to be depicted. Al-Muqaddasī, who was unable to visit Iberia, states that his informants were "a number of Spanish shaykhs."[55]

A similar rigor—or better, religious exclusivism—obtained within the Jewish community. We find the Jewish leadership in Muslim Spain and in the Christian states of the early *Reconquista* boasting of their vigorous action in suppressing the few representatives of the Karaite sect.[56] At the same time that Samuel ha-Nagid was persecuting Karaites in Spain, Rabbanite and Karaite Jews in Egypt, Sicily, and Tunisia were engaged in joint fund-raising campaigns for charity.[57] In eleventh-century Fustat (Old Cairo), the sense of Jewish community was strong enough and broad enough to embrace the Karaites as well—something utterly unthinkable in the Spanish context.

We can understand Samuel ha-Nagid's taking up the cudgel against Karaism in the light of an orthodox mentality that militantly opposed any form of deviation. What is more difficult to explain is his polemical attack against Islam. The Nagid composed a treatise, *sui generis* for that period, pointing out inconsistencies in the text of the Koran.[58] Jewish theological literature frequently contained counterarguments to Muslim attacks on Judaism, but these were mainly *apologiae*, defensive in nature, and were based on Jewish scripture and tradition. Furthermore most of the material containing anti-Muslim polemics was destined for internal Jewish consumption and was cautiously worded.[59] In the rationalist atmosphere of ninth- and tenth-century Baghdad, there seemed to have been rather open discussions and debates between members of the different religions and philosophical schools.[60] In the course of these debates such basic points were raised as the verification of Muḥammad's prophetic mission (*taṣdīq al-nubuwwa*) and the inimitability of the Koran (*iʿjāz al-qurʾān*).[61] These polemics took place within a special intellectual milieu, and the most vehement attacks on either Islam or Judaism came from freethinkers and schismatics from their own respective folds.[62] At any rate there do not seem to have been Jewish equivalents in the Near East to John of Damascus or Theodorus Abū Qūrra.

Samuel ha-Nagid's polemical treatise represents a supreme confidence in his own political position and in his indispensability to the Berber king of Granada. It was also representative of his complete assimilation—strange as that might sound—into Andalusian culture. The Nagid's personality was a perfect blend of that tripartite upper-class pride in the purity of language, lineage, and religion. When asked rhetorically in one of his meditations: "Are you capable of properly praising God?," the Nagid immediately replies: "I answered him, I am the David of my generation."[63]

The Nagid's criticism of the Koran provoked a vehement retort from the great Muslim polygraph Ibn Ḥazm, who, like the Nagid, could include within the scope of his writings love poetry and treatises on grammar, ethics, and theology. In fact Ibn Ḥazm had met Samuel b. Naghrēla and had discussed religion with him when they were both barely twenty years of age. Sometime after that meeting Ibn Ḥazm composed a treatise exposing Jewish and Christian falsification of the Pentateuch and the Gospels (*Izhār tabdīl al-yahūd wa 'l-naṣārā lil-tawrāt wa 'l-injīl*) which was later incorporated into his *Book of Religions and Sects*.[64] Ibn Ḥazm was a very skillful critic of the inconsistencies of the Bible, and it may well be that years later, at the height of his political power, Samuel ha-Nagid decided to repay Ibn Ḥazm's attacks on the Scriptures in kind.

The Nagid, like most of his contemporaries, probably could not see the progressing religious polarization which was taking place in eleventh-century Andalusian society. After all he and his partisans had equally vituperative literary exchanges with the Hebrew grammarian Ibn Janāḥ and his school.[65] The satirical essay of the *muwallad* Ibn García, lampooning the Arabs and praising the native Spanish stock, drew more and equally bitter refutations than his own polemical work.[66] The Nagid's sharp-tongued opponent, Ibn Ḥazm, was forced to live out most of his life as a semirecluse because of his unpopularity with the Muslim civil and religious authorities. Besides it was the very fragmentation of Andalusian society which had up until then afforded the Jews the opportunity to participate in social and political life on a more advantageous and equal footing than anywhere else in the Islamic *oikoumene*. This traditional fragmentation at first probably obscured the religious polarization. The trend, however, was soon to become clear.

Ten years after Samuel ha-Nagid's death, his son and successor Joseph was assassinated, and many of

Granada's Jews were killed in the rioting that ensued. The depth of anti-Jewish resentment, which culminated in the upheaval of 1066, can be seen from the rabble-rousing poetry of Abū Isḥāq of Elvira.[67]

The loss of Toledo in 1085 to Alfonso VI of Leon and Castile and the incorporation of most of al-Andalus into the Almoravid empire after 1090 had the effect of sharpening religious and ethnic distinctions. Despite some erosion of Jewish status, life under the Almoravids continued more or less along the lines of the preceding century. There was, to be sure, a progressive decline in the number of Jews in the civil service, and there were no longer any personalities wielding political authority comparable to the Ibn Naghrēlas or Yequtiel b. Ḥasan in the preceding century. Nonetheless there were still peripheral court figures. More important, the exquisitely refined lifestyle of the upper class of merchants, scholars, and courtiers remained unchanged. From the Cairo Geniza documents from this period, we see that "in Spain, even a humdrum business letter . . . was preceded by a carefully worded introduction, mostly in rhymed prose. The superlative epithets contained in it can be rendered in English only very imperfectly."[68]

Spanish Jews were still quite active in Mediterranean trade during the Almoravid period. The Geniza has preserved a partnership contract between the widely traveled India merchant Ḥalfōn b. Nathanel and the Spanish poet Judah b. Ghiyāth.[69] Judah ha-Levi was a close friend of both these men, and in one Geniza letter he appears as a silent partner in one of Ḥalfōn b. Nethanel's business ventures.[70]

Andalusian Jewry could still be justifiably proud of its religious scholarship. The *yeshiva* founded by the great talmudist Isaac al-Fāsī in Lucena continued to

flourish under his pupil Joseph b. Migash (d. 1141).
Both have left behind a wealth of legal *responsa*.[71]

Some Jews moved to the Christian North. After the
second destruction of Granadan Jewry in 1090, Moses
b. Ezra went into wandering in Christian Spain. In
numerous poems he complains of the bitterness of exile
from the cultured south:

> I am with them a gentleman amongst savages
> And a lion amidst a flock of apes and parrots.

Jewish civilization in Muslim Spain still showed all
the vital life signs. In retrospect it was clearly be-
coming somewhat tired. Here and there we find individuals intensely concerned with messianism. The
renewed vigor of the *Reconquista*, the Almoravid invasion, and the cataclysmic events of the First Crusade
seemed to many to be the "Pangs of the Messiah."[72]

The optimism of earlier philosophical speculation
with its inherent faith in the human intellect and the
primacy of reason gave way in some quarters to pietist
withdrawal. In Baḥya b. Paqūda's *Duties of the Heart*
(written ca. 1075), the ultimate communion with God
is reached via the *ṣufī* path, not that of the philosophers.[73] The soul is purified by spiritual exercises
and thus released from the bonds of sensuality. Baḥya's
retreat into mystic piety was by no means universal.
His Muslim contemporary Ibn Bājja (Avempace)
maintained quite to the contrary that union of the soul
with God could be achieved by an intellectual as-
cent.[74] The unalienated majority of the upper class
probably felt a greater kinship to Ibn Bājja's philosophical intellectuality than to Baḥya's simple piety.
Indeed a new philosophical trend was coming into

vogue in al-Andalus at this time, a trend toward strict Aristotelianism, which drew, among others, upon the work of al-Fārābī, who lived in the East two centuries earlier.[75] All of these polarities must have caused agonizing internal stress within those individuals who had neither detached themselves from the mundane world in order to pass away in *unio mystica*, nor had given themselves over to a philosophical relativism that held that all religious symbols point to the same ultimate truth as philosophical knowledge.

One such individual was the physician and poet Abu ʾl-Ḥasan Judah ha-Levi. He resided sometimes in the Muslim South and sometimes in Christian-held Toledo, which was a point of osmosis between two civilizations.[76] Ha-Levi had been a youthful prodigy and was recognized and encouraged by such men as Moses b. Ezra, while the latter was still in Granada. By the time he had reached maturity, he was acknowledged the undisputed master of his art. His poetry shows that he possessed a sparkling wit and a polished grace.

Somewhere along the way, Judah ha-Levi began to go through a spiritual crisis that must have been experienced by others of his generation. The crisis is documented in his sublime religious poems. Nearly all his predecessors had written prayers for Israel's redemption. Yet when I read Samual ha-Nagid's religious poetry, for example, and this is, of course, entirely impressionistic—I do not find the same burning intensity or painful immediacy.[77]

At one point Judah ha-Levi is given over to the apocalyptic speculation to which I referred above. In a poem of haunting alliteration he relates a dream in which it was revealed to him that the dominion of

Islam would pass away in the year 1130.[78] In Fez, R. Moses Darʿī, who had studied in Spain with Ibn Migash, declared that the Messiah would appear during the very same year.[79] Many must have been sorely disappointed when 1130 came and went.

The failure of apocalyptic messianism cast many into doubt and despair. The dark night of ha-Levi's soul found expression in his sombre penitential poems (selīḥōt). Like the great Muslim theologian al-Ghazālī (d. 1111) in the East, Judah ha-Levi recovered from this bitter interlude and at last reached a deep spiritual certainty. This next stage in his pilgrim's progress is reflected in the sublime poetic series, usually referred to as the Zionides, and his philosophical dialogue The Kuzari.

He had begun The Kuzari in the preceding decade, partially as a traditional response to Karaism, but had been dissatisfied with the effort.[80] It was only after overcoming his own crisis of faith, and indeed in response to it, that he recast and expanded the work into its final form. The Kuzari is not only a glorification of rabbinic Judaism, "An Apology for the Despised Religion," but it is also an unabashed statement of nationalism, very much in the modern sense of the word. The elements upon which ha-Levi's nationalism is built would be familiar to any student of the phenomenon—race, language, soil, historical experience and destiny, and romanticism, which is ultimately a rejection of rationalism. Of course several of these were also components of the Spanish exclusivism which we discussed earlier. But Judah ha-Levi's emphasis and the conclusions which he drew were totally different.

"Palestine," says the Rabbi in The Kuzari (Book V, 23), "has a special relation to the Lord of Israel. Pure life can be perfect only there." The Rabbi goes on to explain why he shall leave the land of the Khazars to go to Palestine:

> I seek freedom—from the service of those numerous people only whose favour I shall never obtain even if I work for it all my life and which would not profit me, even if I could obtain it: I mean the service of men and the courting of their favour.   —(*Kuzari* V, 25)

What Judah ha-Levi was saying—and his compatriots understood him perfectly well—was that the Andalusian civilization of which they were so proud was vanity and that the prestige, influence, and all the efforts of the Jewish upper class were for naught. It was, moreover, a waste of time to try to transplant Andalusian Jewry to the Christian kingdoms of Northern Spain. In *The Kuzari* Judah ha-Levi had rejected the whole ethos of their culture. In his view philosophy had failed in the metaphysical sphere. The cosmopolitan intellectuals of al-Andalus were deluding themselves if they thought that their harmonious synthesis of philosophy and religion, of Arabic culture and Jewish tradition, could provide the ideal life. Judging from the reaction of his Spanish contemporaries, most did not agree.

Not long afterwards Judah ha-Levi, in spite of his age and the protestations of his friends, left Spain for Egypt and thence Palestine, where he died in July 1141.

By 1172 the Almohads had taken almost complete control of Islamic Spain and Jewish life ceased to exist. Many Andalusian Jews found a haven in the North both for themselves and for their culture. Through them and their coreligionists in Provence an important body of the cultural heritage of Islamic Spain and of the Arabic-speaking world in general was to be transmitted to Latin Europe.

We have now come full circle and returned to our starting point. As I began with a quote from Judah ha-Levi, I would like to conclude with his farewell verse to a Spanish traveling companion who had accompanied him to Egypt:

and this is the last of all my friends from Spain.[81]

NOTES

1. Samuel ha-Nagid, *Divan Shmuel Hanagid*, ed. Dov Jarden (Jerusalem, 1966), 81, vss. 9–17.

2. Cf. A. S. Halkin, "Le-Tōledōt ha-Shemad bīmē hā-al-Muwaḥḥidīn," *Joshua Starr Memorial Volume* New York, 1953), pp. 101–10; H. Z. Hirschberg, *A History of the Jews in North Africa* I (Jerusalem, 1965), pp. 84–102; Roger Le Tourneau, *The Almohad Movement in North Africa in the Twelfth and Thirteenth Centuries* (Princeton, 1969), pp. 57f and 77. For an attempt which is not altogether convincing at a revisionist treatment of the Almohad persecution, cf. David Corcos, "Le-Ofī Yaḥasām shel Shelīṭē ha-al-Muwaḥḥadūn Līhūdīm," *Zion* 32 (1967): 137–60, where there is, however, an excellent review of the bibliography.

3. For the possible identification of biblical Tarshish with Spain, cf. S. R. Driver, *An Introduction to the Literature of the Old Testament* (New York, 1916), p. 321.

4. Henri Pirenne, *Mohammed and Charlemagne* (Cleveland & New York, 1965), pp. 79–86.

5. For a full treatment of Visigothic Jewish policy, cf. Bernard S. Bachrach, "A Reassessment of Visigothic Jewish Policy, 589–711," *American Historical Review* 78, 1 (February 1973): 11–34.

6. Cf. B. Lewis, "An Apocalyptic Vision of Islamic History," *Bulletin of the School of Oriental and African Studies of the University of London* 13 (1950): 308–38.

7. Cf. Bachrach, "A Reassessment of Visigothic Jewish Policy," p. 30. Some Spanish historians even up until the present century have maintained that Jews not only plotted with their brethren in North Africa, but indeed did hand over Spain to the Muslims. Cf., e.g., J. Amador de los Rios, *Historia social, política y religiosa de los judíos de España y Portugal* (Madrid, 1875), p. 107, and A. Ballesteros y Beretta, *Historia de España y su influencia en la historia universal* II (Barcelona, 1914), p. 107.

8. For Jewish collaboration in Elvira, cf. the anonymous Arabic chronicle *Akhbār Majmūʿa*, ed. E. Lafuente y Alcántara (Madrid, 1867), p. 12; in Cordova, *ibid.*, p. 14; in Toledo, cf. Ibn ʿIdhārī, *al-Bayān al-Mughrib fī Akhbār al-Andalus wa ʾl-Maghrib* II, ed. G. S. Colin & E. Lévi-Provençal (Leiden, 1951), p. 12. For other sources, including the Latin, cf. E. Ashtor, *Qōrōt ha-Yehūdīm Bisfārād ha-Mūslimīt* I (Jerusalem, 1966), pp. 9–13 and the notes, pp. 269–71; Eng. tr., *The Jews of Moslem Spain* I (Philadelphia, 1973), pp. 15–22, and pp. 407–08, n. 1–10.

9. al-Balādhurī, *Futūh al-Buldān* (Cairo, 1959), p.

147; English translation by P. Hitti, *The Origins of the Islamic State* (New York, 1916), p. 217.

10. Cf. Claude Cahen, "Dhimma," *Encylopedia of Islam* II new edition (Leiden, 1974), 227–31.

11. *Patrologia Latina* 98, 385.

12. Cf. e.g., the incident cited in S. D. Goitein, *A Mediterranean Society* I (Berkeley & Los Angeles, 1967), p. 136. There were, however, examples of Muslim converts to Judaism in the Middle Ages. Cf. *ibid.* II, pp. 303–11.

13. Cf. Ashtor, *Qōrōt ha-Yehūdīm* I, p. 52, and the sources cited on p. 274, n. 18; Engl. tr. pp. 73 and 412, n. 18.

14. Cf. *ibid.*, pp. 52–55; Eng. tr. pp. 74–79.

15. Perhaps he suggested such a course of action vis à vis the Judaizing heretics. Concerning the argument over the interpretation of "cingulum militiae," cf. B. Blumenkrantz, "Du nouveau sur Bodo-Eléazar?", *Revue des Études Juives* 112 (1953): 39 and Ashtor, *Qōrōt ha-Yehūdīm* I, pp. 51 and 247, n. 17; Eng. tr. pp. 72 and 412, n. 17.

16. Montgomery Watt, *A History of Islamic Spain* (with additional sections on literature by Pierre Cachia), *Islamic Surveys* 4 (Edinburgh, 1965), p. 57.

17. Cf. E. Lévi-Provençal, *Histoire de l'Espagne musulmane* I (Paris, 1950), p. 239.

18. al-Maqrīzī, *al-Mawāʿiz wa ʾl-Iʿtibār fī Dhikr al-Khiṭaṭ wa ʾl-Āthār* I (Bulaq, 1853), p. 424; Nāsir-i Khosraw *Safar Nāme* (Berlin, 1341 A.H.), pp. 81f; and Ibn Muyassar, *Taʾrīkh Miṣr* (Cairo, 1919), p. 3.

19. al-Maqqarī, *Nafḥ al-Ṭīb* (*Annalectes sur l'histoire et la littérature des Arabes d'Espagne*) II, ed. R.

Dozy et al. (1855–1861), pp. 83–90, especially p. 85.

20. Ashtor, *Qōrōt ha-Yehūdīm* I, postulates three large waves of Jewish immigration into Spain. This may be so, but there was a continuous East-West flow of people in the Islamic world until the Fatimid conquest of Egypt in 969, when there began a new West-East movement which would continue into the twelfth century. Cf. N. A. Stillman, *East-West Relations in the Islamic Mediterranean in the Early Eleventh Century* (Ph.D. dissertation, University of Pennsylvania, Philadelphia, 1970), pp. 1f.

21. Ashtor, *Qōrōt ha-Yehūdīm* I, pp. 82f; Eng. tr. p. 119ff.

22. See Benjamin M. Lewin, *From the Gaonic Period 2: The Epistle of R. Sherira Gaon* (Haifa, 1921), p. 104 (in Hebrew); Judah b. Barzillay, *Sēfer hā-ʿIttīm*, ed. J. Schorr (Cracow, 1903), p. 267. This event has been confused with two other important events which took place at approximately the same time: i.e., Charlemagne's inviting a member of the Kalonymos family of Lucca to come to Mayence and the arrival of the Babylonian scholar Makhir in Narbonne in 802. Cf. Salo Baron, *A Social and Religious History of the Jews* V (New York, 1957), pp. 46f.

23. Louis Ginzberg, *Geonica* I (repr. New York, 1968), p. 121. As to the contents of *Sēder R. ʿAmram Gaon*, cf. *ibid.*, pp. 123–50.

24. Carl Brockelmann, *Geschichte der arabischen Literatur* Supplementband I (Leiden, 1945–1949), p. 251.

25. S. D. Goitein, *Studies in Islamic History and Institutions* (Leiden, 1966), pp. 54–70.

26. Ṣāʿid al-Andalusī, *Kitāb Ṭabaqāt al-Umam*, ed. L. Cheikho (Beirut, 1912), pp. 88f. French tr. by R. Blachère (Paris, 1935), p. 158. Ibn Abī Uṣaybiʿa, *ʿUyūn al-Anbāʾ fī Ṭabaqāt al-Aṭibbāʾ*, ed. Nizār Riḍā (Beirut, 1965), pp. 494 and 498. Ibn Abī Uṣaybiʿa borrows heavily from Ṣāʿid.

27. Ibn Abī Uṣaybiʿa, *ʿUyun al-Anba*, p. 494. His source here is Ibn Juljul, a younger contemporary of Ḥasday's. Cf. also Lucien Leclerc, *Histoire de la médecine arabe* I (Paris, 1876), p. 419.

28. Ibn Daud, *Sēfer ha-Qabbalah*, ed. and tr. by G. Cohen (Philadelphia, 1967), p. 49, l. 50 (Heb. text); p. 67, l. 73 (Eng. tr.), calls Ḥasday "the great *nasi*." Concerning *nasis* in the Middle East, cf. Goitein, *A Mediterranean Society* II, p. 19.

29. Ed. H. Filipowski (London, 1854).

30. Cf. A. Mirsky, " ʿArkhē ha-Shīrā hā-ʿIvrīt bi-Sfārād," in *The Spanish Heritage* I, ed. R. Bennet (New York, 1971), pp. 186–268. Cf. also, Jefim (Hayyim) Schirmann, *Ha-Shīrā hā-ʿIvrīt biSfārād ūve-Prōvāns* I (Jerusalem & Tel Aviv, 1961), pp. xxiii–iv, and *ibid.*, pp. 701–37.

31. Ibn Daud, *Sēfer ha-Qabbalah*, p. 73 (Heb.), p. 102 (Eng.).

32. Gerson D. Cohen, "The Story of the Four Captives," *Proceedings of the American Academy for Jewish Research* 29 (1960–1961): 55–131.

33. Ibn Daud, *Sēfer ha-Qabbalah*, p. 48 (Heb.), p. 66 (Eng.); cf. Cohen's notes, p. 135.

34. *Ibid.*, Cohen's notes, p. 135.

35. Ṣāʿid al-Andalusī, *Kitāb*, pp. 88f (Ar. text); p. 159 (Fr. tr.).

36. TS 20.100, 11. 23–25, ed. Jacob Mann, *Texts and Studies in Jewish History and Literature* I (repr. New York, 1972), p. 121.

37. Baron, *History of the Jews* V, pp. 46f.

38. Samuel A. Poznanski, "Anshē Qayrawān," in *Festschrift zu Ehren des Dr. A. Harkavy* (St. Petersburg, 1908), pp. 175–220; Goitein, *A Mediterranean Society*, vols. I and II, passim; *idem.*, *Studies*, pp. 308–28; and N. A. Stillman, "Quelques renseignements biographiques sur Joseph Ibn ʿAwkal, un médiateur entre les communautés juives du Maghreb et les Académies d'Irak," to appear in *Revue des Études Juives* 132, 4 (October–December, 1973): 529–42.

39. Cf. Stillman, *East-West Relations*, pp. 41–46.

40. Cf. n. 39. Baron seems to overgeneralize, but he may be right as far as Spain is concerned.

41. For a comprehensive treatment of the poetry of the period, cf. Henri Pérès, *La poésie andalouse en arabe classique* (Paris, 1953). In addition to the studies cited in n. 32, cf. Jefim Schirmann, "The Function of the Hebrew Poet in Medieval Spain," *Jewish Social Studies* 16, 3 (July 1954): 235–52.

42. S. D. Goitein, *Studies in Bible* (Tel Aviv, 1963), p. 59 (in Hebrew).

43. Nehemia Allony, "The 'Zevi' (Nasib) in the Hebrew Poetry in Spain," *Sefarad* 23, Fascicle 2 (1963): 311–21. Jefim Schirmann, "The Ephebe in Medieval Hebrew Poetry," *Sefarad* 15, Fascicle 1 (1955): 55–68.

44. S. D. Goitein, "Formal Friendship in the Medieval Near East," *Proceedings of the American*

Philosophical Society 115, 6 (December 1971): 489.

45. *Rōsh ha-Shānā* 25b. Cf. also Goitein, *Studies*, pp. 197–213 for Jewish and Islamic attitudes towards government.

46. Cf. Cohen's analysis in his edition of Ibn Daud, *Sēfer ha-Qabbalah*, pp. 278–89.

47. Cf. the poems in Jacob Mann, *The Jews in Egypt and in Palestine Under the Fātimid Caliphs* II (repr. New York, 1970), pp. 11–13, 75–77, or 207.

48. Cf. A. J. Arberry, *Arabic Poetry* (Cambridge, 1965), pp. 86 (Eng. tr.) and 87 (Ar. text), vs. 24: "You surpassed the bounds of courage and reason/So that people said you *had knowledge of the unseen*." Compare this with Suras 39:46, 59:22, 64:18, and 72:26 (to give but a few examples).

49. Pérès, *La poésie andalouse*, pp. 269f. This poem is a remarkable piece of sycophancy, even considering its genre. It is surprising that Pérès and after him A. R. Nykl, *Hispano-Arabic Poetry* (Baltimore, 1946), p. 200, should believe the poet's claim to practice Judaism secretly amongst his fellow Muslims.

50. Moses b. Ezra, *Sēfer Shīrat Yisrā'ēl* (Kitāb al-Muhādara wa 'l-Mudhākara), tr. to Hebrew by B. Halper (Jerusalem, 5727), p. 62.

51. *Ibid.*, p. 53.

52. al-Harīzī, *Tahkemōnī*, ed. Y. Toporovsky (Tel Aviv, 1952), p. 12.

53. Cf. Américo Castro, *The Structure of Spanish History* (Princeton, 1954) and most recently, *idem.*, *The Spaniards* (Berkeley & Los Angeles, 1971), especially Chaps. III, VII, and VIII.

54. al-Muqaddasī, *Ahsan al-Taqāsīm fī Ma'rifat al-*

Aqālīm, ed. M. J. De Goeje (Leiden, 1906), p. 236.

55. *Ibid.*, p. 237. On Shāfiʿism and Ẓāhirism in Spain, cf. Lévi-Provençal, *L'Espagne musulmane* III, pp. 476–79; and on Muʿtazilism, *ibid.*, pp. 480–85.

56. Judah b. Barzillay, *Sēfer hā-ʿIttīm*, p. 267; Ibn Daud, *Sēfer ha-Qabbalah*, pp. 69–72 (Heb. text) and pp. 94–101 (Eng. tr.).

57. Cf. e.g., TS 13 J 8, f. 14, a summary of which is given by Goitein, *A Mediterranean Society*, II, p. 472. Cf. also *ibid.*, p. 7.

58. Extracts of the treatise survive in the refutation of Ibn Ḥazm. Cf. E. García-Gómez, "Polémica religiosa entre Ibn Hazm e Ibn al-Nagrila," *al-Andalus* 4 (1936): 1–28. Cf. also, M. Perlmann, "Eleventh-century Andalusian Authors on the Jews of Granada," *PAAJR* 18 (1948–1949): 280–84.

59. The basic bibliographical source for the polemical literature is M. Steinschneider, *Polemische und apologetische Literatur in arabischer Sprache zwischen Muslimen, Christen und Juden* (Leipzig, 1877). This was followed by two excellent studies: I. Goldziher, "Über muhammedanische Polemik gegen Ahl al-Kitāb," *Zeitschrift des Deutschen Morgenländischen Gesellschaft* 32 (1878), and M. Schreiner, "Zur Geschichte der Polemik zwischen Juden und Muhammedanern," *ZDMG* 42 (1888).

60. Cf. the often-quoted passage from al-Ḥumaydī's *Jadhwat al-Muqtabis*, e.g., in A. Altmann, *Three Jewish Philosophers* (New York, 1969), part. 2, pp. 13–14.

61. Cf. Schreiner, *ZDMG* 42, pp. 663–75. There

is an extensive literature on *nubuwwa* and *i'jāz al-qur'ān* which had not been edited in Schreiner's day. This will be treated by my student, Mr. Richard Martin, in a thesis dealing with an eleventh-century commentary of Ibn Khallād's *Kitāb al-Uṣūl*.

62. From such men as Abū Bakr al-Rāzī and Ibn al-Rawandī for Islam and Ḥīwī al-Balkhī and Ibn Sāqawayh for Judaism.

63. Samuel ha-Nagid, *Divan*, p. 33, vs. 38; also in Schirmann, *ha-Shīrā hā-'Ivrīt* I, p. 111.

64. Cf. Perlmann, *PAAJR* 18, 270–79.

65. Cf. Joseph and Hartwig Derenbourg's introduction to *Opuscules et traités d'Abou 'l-Walid Merwan Ibn Djanah de Cordoue* (Paris, 1880), pp. i–lix. Cf. also the sources cited by Schirmann, "Samuel Hannagid, the Man, the Soldier, the Politician," *Jewish Social Studies* 13, 2 (April 1951): 116, nn. 70–73.

66. Cf. James T. Monroe, *The Shu'ūbiyya in Al-Andalus: The Risāla of Ibn García and Five Refutations* (Berkeley & Los Angeles, 1970). Monroe's analysis of the conflict between orthodoxy and liberal heterodoxy in the introductory essay should be approached with extreme caution.

67. The text of this poem was published by R. Dozy, *Recherches sur l'histoire et la littérature de l'Espagne* I, 3rd edition (Leiden, 1881), pp. LXIII–LXVIII. Its contents are summarized in English by Perlmann, *PAAJR* 18, 284–88.

68. S. D. Goitein, *Letters of Medieval Jewish Traders* (Princeton, 1973), p. 260.

69. This document will be published by Professor Goitein in his forthcoming *India Book*, No. 115.

70. Cf. Bodl. MS Heb. d 74, f. 41 (*India Book*, No.

104); translated in Goitein, *Jewish Traders*, pp. 260–63. Cf. also Goitein, "The Biography of Rabbi Judah ha-Levi in the Light of the Cairo Geniza Documents," *PAAJR* 28 (1959): 41–56.

71. The printed editions of their *responsa* are listed in A. I. Laredo, "Las ʿŠěelot u-Tešubot ʾ como fuente para la historia de los Judios Españoles," *Sefarad* 5, Fascicle 2 (1945): 453–54.

72. Cf. Baron, *Jews* V, pp. 138–208, especially pp. 150–59 and 199–203. Concerning Judah ha-Levi's messianism, cf. Schirmann, *ha-Shīrā hā-ʿIvrīt* II, pp. 428–429 and 480.

73. Baḥya b. Paqūda, *Kitāb al-Hidāya ilā Farāʾiḍ al-Qulūb*, ed. A. S. Yahuda (Leiden, 1912). The most complete study of Baḥya's relation to Islamic pietism is Georges Vajda, *La théologie ascétique de Bahja ibn Paquda* (Paris, 1947).

74. Cf. S. Munk, *Mélanges de la philosophie juive et arabe* (Paris, 1927), pp. 389–409, where a summary is given of Ibn Bājja's *Fī Tadbīr al-Mutawaḥḥid* (*On the Rule of the Solitary*) from the Hebrew translation of Moses of Narbonne.

75. Cf. Richard Walzer, *Greek into Arabic* (Cambridge, Mass., 1962), pp. 18–23 and especially, 26–28.

76. For the biography of Judah ha-Levi, cf. David Kaufmann, *Studies in Hebrew Literature of the Middle Ages* (in Hebrew), tr. I. Eldad (Jerusalem, 5725), pp. 166–207; J. Schirmann, "The Life of Jehuda ha-Levi," *Tarbiz* 9 (1937–1938): 35–54, 219–240, 284–305 (in Hebrew); and the important article of Goitein, cited in note 70.

77. Compare, for example, the poems of Samuel ha-Nagid in Schirmann, *ha-Shīrā hā-ʿIvrīt* I, pp.

146f and the brief poem of Judah ha-Levi in *ibid.* II, top of p. 481.

78. Schirmann, *ha-Shīrā hā-ʿIvrīt*, p. 480.

79. Maimonides, *Epistle to Yemen*, ed. A. S. Halkin (New York, 1952), pp. 100–102. Cf. Baron, *Jews* V, p. 201f. Most of Darʿī's followers were ruined financially.

80. Goitein, in *PAAJR* 28 (1959): 46ff.

81. *Diwan*, ed. H. Brody (Berlin, 1896–1897), vol. I, p. 13, No. XI.

TWO PARALLEL MEDIEVAL COMMONPLACES: ANTIFEMINISM AND ANTISEMITISM IN THE HISPANIC LITERARY TRADITION

Harriet Goldberg

Before undertaking the task of pointing out the similarities between the phenomena of antifeminism and antisemitism in the Hispanic medieval literary tradition, I must make a few disclaimers. It is not my intention to make any value judgments, nor do I intend to suggest that the examples adduced in this study are evidence from which sociological or historical conclusions might be drawn. Different sources would have to be used to establish the quality of life in Spain for either Jews or women. As a measure of the heat and emotion which both topics engender, we might consider the fact that Isidore Epstein quotes Graetz to the effect that outside of Spain:

> . . . there was often to be found nothing more than a chaotic welter of all the dark forces of medieval barbarism and monarchal fanaticism let loose

against the unfortunate children of Israel; in Spain
they enjoyed much personal respect and basked in
the sun of tolerance.[1]

On the other hand Arthur Lukyn Williams writes: "For
Spain stands out above all countries for the suffering
of the Jews, inflicted, alas, by those who called themselves Christians."[2] Some Hispanists indulge in the ex-
culpatory tactic of observing that, since the laws for
Jews and Moors were nearly equal, there was little or no
Spanish antisemitism. Kenneth R. Scholberg asserts in
response to this notion: "Even though Islam was a
greater threat to Christianity than was Judaism, hatred
was more pronounced against the Israelites than against
the Saracens." He sees special significance that "accusa-
tions of ritual murder or of sacrilegious parodies were
leveled against one group and not the other."[3] Fernando
Rubio Álvarez suggests that eastern literature was the
source of any antifeminist sentiment in Hispanic letters
and that only in Scripture and in Christian literature is
the woman treated fairly, an observation that even the
most casual reader might find questionable.[4] Much of
the literature I intend to examine falls into the didactic
category whose declared purpose was to instruct and
delight the reader. For the most part these works were
intended to reinforce already established positions
rather than to introduce new ones.

It is hardly necessary to establish the existence of the
two attitudes in medieval Spain—Barbara Matulka,
María Pilar del Oñate, and Jacob Ornstein have dealt
with the profeminism/antifeminism controversy in
Spain. An additional commentary is to be found in my
study of the fifteenth-century profeminist work, Fray
Martín de Córdoba's *Jardín de nobles donzellas*.[5] Fernando Rubio Álvarez includes the *cancioneros* with their

abundance of doctrinal matter in his study.[6] Hispanic antisemitism is described by Adolfo de Castro, José Amador de los Ríos, Solomon Katz, Arthur Lukyn Williams, Yitzhak Baer, Abraham Neuman, Israel Epstein, Bernard Bachrach, and James Parkes.[7]

As a starting point out of the mass of generalities about prejudice, we might posit for the sake of convenience the following definition: "We invent a justifiable and respectable reason for our true motives and feelings and equally a disreputable and discreditable reason for the activities of the minority."[8] The activities referred to in the definition will be considered as they are described in the Hispanic tradition either in connection with women or with Jews. The three principal areas are: lasciviousness, treachery, and involvement with the devil. First, both groups were thought to be sexually insatiable, practicing the ancillary sins of intemperance, gluttony, and drunkenness. They were thought to be treacherous, disloyal, and frequently deceitful in their dealings with others, which often led to their being stingy, avaricious, envious, and covetous. Both groups were said to be arms of the devil, and in consequence sacrilegious; they were practicers of witchcraft and capable of remarkable depravities. In connection with this last category both women and Jews suffered from *superbia*, that arrogant pride which so dismayed their neighbors. Neither group was ever accused of stupidity; their error was willful intractability, or obstinacy.

Other similarities will emerge, but the central one is that both groups represented perils that threatened to weaken, damage, or even destroy the faith of a good Christian man. Is it necessary to establish to any reader of patristic or exemplary literature that the Church had two enemies or adversaries besides Satan—women and Jews? In the exemplary tradition woman appears as the temptress, whose very existence threatens the upright, devout ascetic.[9] *Exempla*, used as illustrative material in sermons, made palatable the weighty admonitions from such sources as St. Jerome and St. Ambrose. In speaking of the elect, St. Jerome writes: "These are they who have not defiled themselves with woman, for they continued virgins."[10] St. Ambrose, whose praises of virgins and chaste widows were widely read, describes woman as a weapon of the devil to capture men's souls in *Concerning Repentance*.[11] The logic is clear; sexuality is most easily condemned by attacking the temptation rather than the tempted.

In order to see the Jew as adversary, it is not necessary to resort to such blatantly vituperative examples of anti-Jewish sentiment as the *Adversus Judaeos* of St. John Chrysostom—even so reasonable a philosopher as St. Augustine found it necessary to explain that angels were not mentioned in the Old Testament because Moses, the author of the Pentateuch, could not reveal their existence to a people who were carnal. The carnality of the Jews was expressed in their petitions to God for such trivialities as good crops, many sons, and victory over their enemies, rather than petitions for more spiritual benefits.[12] In any case the preservation and defense of the faith is clearly the "justifiable and respectable reason" mentioned in our definition. With this reason in hand, most expressions of antifeminism and antisemitism could be justified, if they were to be challenged.

Two scholars on the subject of antisemitism have expressed divergent, but not mutually exclusive, opinions about the origin of Christian antipathy toward the Jew, each of which is equally applicable to Christian antipathy toward women as well. James Parkes writes that the conflict between "right-minded and wrong-minded peoples" stemmed from "the picture created in patristic literature of the Jew as a being perpetually betraying God and ultimately abandoned by Him."[13] If we need to confirm the existence of this attitude in the Hispanic tradition, we can refer to the *Primera crónica general*, written under the aegis of Alfonso X el Sabio at the end of the thirteenth century. It is explained there that Titus had ordered the burning of Jerusalem because the Jews had killed Jesus and, thus, their national identity was destroyed in accordance with earlier prophecies which they had ignored.[14] The betrayal of God and abandonment by Him appear together as though they were an established formulaic expression.

Obviously it is not possible to assert that misogyny stemmed only from patristic or Christian polemic condemnations of women. Nevertheless women were regularly pointed out as potentially dangerous, damaging creatures. They not only tempted celibates, causing them to misbehave, or at the very least to harbor impure thoughts, but they also caused their husbands much difficulty because of their deceitful ways. Certainly the *exempla* describing this kind of feminine activity enlivened and reinforced the more serious antifeminism of elevated theological sources.[15]

The second scholarly statement on the subject of antisemitism which we can use is that of Marcel Simon, who views Christian antipathy toward Jews as a continuation of Greco-Roman anti-Christianism. He attributes this hostility as a response to Jewish refusal to accept the truth about God.[16]

Feminine separatism, aloofness, or inscrutability is a misogynistic cliché. Alfonso Martínez de Toledo observed in his jocular *Arcipreste de Talavera* (1438) that no matter how familiar, intimate, or friendly a man may be with a woman, he will never know her secrets. There will always be a secret corner of her heart not subject to his will or control.[17]

Having established the groundwork for this polemical parallel, the stereotypes can be examined one at a time, beginning with the excessive sexuality of the two groups, continuing with their treachery, and finally discussing the most serious allegation of all, their alliance with the Devil, with all its attendant depravity. As these three parallel stereotypes—sexuality, treachery, and demonism—are examined, we can apply the perspectives of Parkes and of Simon: Jews and women were despised because the Church Fathers found them to be culpable in the betrayal of God and his servants, and because the two groups held themselves apart or aloof from the mainstream of society; in short they were guilty of separatism.

Excessive sexuality is a frequent accusation in intergroup prejudice. It is not surprising to find the allegation in the antisemitic tradition. The notion that the Jews were a particularly lascivious people found support in Hosea 9:11, in which Hosea complains about his faithless wife and her whorish ways (a metaphor for the Jewish people who were whoring after false gods), and Jeremiah 3:3, 7:11, and 12:7, which used the same metaphor. Even in its most literal, modern interpretation, Hosea is considered to be the expression of love even in the face of ingratitude.[18] However St. John Chrysostom made use of these passages, calling the synagogue a brothel and a den of thieves, and, following the concatenated scheme of sins, points out that according to Moses the Jews were also given to overeating and overdrinking with the result that they were all obese.[19]

In addition to the literary excesses of the authors of Jeremiah and Hosea, the opinion that Jews were sexually overactive seems to have been based, in part, on the necessity to explain the differences in the marriage and divorce laws of the Jews and of the Christians. In the *Dialogue of St. Justin Martyr with Trypho the Jew* Justin admonishes Trypho:

> It would be better for you to follow God than your foolish and blind teachers, who permit you even now to have four or five wives each; and if any of you see a handsome woman and desire her, they recount the actions of Jacob. . . .[20]

Isidore Epstein points out that Spanish Jews continued to practice polygamy as late as the thirteenth century, particularly in the case of the first wife's sterility.[21]

Leviratic marriages might have made non-Jews uneasy, but the apparent ease of Jewish divorce must have been an even more provocative issue. In 1468 Fray Martín de Córdoba asserted that the Old Law permitted bills of divorcement because Jews were so hard-hearted that they might kill their unwanted wives if they were not permitted to divorce them.[22] Also in fifteenth-century Spain we find the epithet *adúlteros* applied to Jews in a sort of formulaic catalogue of their faults in which they were also called covetous, disloyal, unfaithful, and sowers of discord.[23]

To complete the portrait of the Jew as a sexual peril we can refer to the proposed legal code prepared under the direction of Alfonso X el Sabio in the thirteenth century, which dealt with the penalties to be exacted in cases of intermarriage or sexual interaction between Jews and Christians. The *Siete Partidas* and their first draft, the *Setenario*, were really only quasi-legal documents when they were prepared. In spite of Alfonso's intentions they served for almost a hundred years as nothing more than a treatise on government, not as a

legal code. Just as many states in the United States of
America had laws forbidding miscegenation, Jewish-
Christian marriages were first forbidden in the fourth
century at the Council of Elvira. In the *Siete Partidas*
the Jewish male participant in such a union suffered the
same penalty as the adulterer—death. His Christian
lady-friend, either virgin or widow, was to lose half her
possessions for the first offense and all of them for the
second (*Partida* VII, *título* xxiv, *ley* 9, III, 674). A
married woman could be burned if her husband desired
it; she could also be set free or punished in any way her
husband chose if she indulged in this activity (*Partida*
VII, *título* xxvi, *ley* 10) and if she were a woman who
ordinarily made herself available to the general public;
both offenders were to be flogged for the first offense
and put to death for the second (*Partida* VII, *título*
xxvi, *ley* 10). Apparently no official notice was to be
taken when a Christian man might cohabit with a Jewish woman except insofar as the rights of inheritance of
the offspring were concerned.[24]

Similarly women were considered the cause of adultery and were generally condemned in sermons dealing
with the importance of celibacy, abstinence, and tem-
perate behavior. The Church first forbade marriages between Jews and Christians, as we have noted, at the
Council of Elvira (ca. 303–306), and interestingly
enough at this same council (held in Spain) clerical
celibacy was first enjoined. Although the initial injunction was not based on the necessity to avoid a morally
reprehensible activity, little by little the emphasis shifted
until woman, a sexually insatiable creature, was seen as
the provocation which the ordinarily decent clergy could
not resist. She also undermined the structure of society
when her unquenchable desires led her to deceive her
husband, since obviously no one man could bring her to

a state of satiety. Is this another indication of her separatism and aloofness to which we have already alluded?
The idea of her insatiability became a commonplace. In
the *Historia de Segundo*, a thirteenth-century didactic
work, we find the definition of the term woman given
in a more or less ritualistic fashion.[25] To the rhetorical
question—"what is woman?", the answer is "man's confusion [in the sense that she will lead him astray], a
beast that is never sated, distress that never goes away,
unceasing war, limitless danger."[26] Elsewhere her lust is
likened to the uncontrollable force of a runaway horse,
unless, of course, she learns to apply the restraints which
God has given her.[27] We find the same concatenation of
lust and wine in misogynistic literature, as we did with
the Jews. Alfonso Martínez de Toledo devotes a chapter
to the damage wine does to a woman. He asks the question whether any woman, be she a maiden, nun, or
widow, married or betrothed, would be unable to deny
her body to any one who desired it if she were *caliente
del vino o turbado*.[28] Fray Martín de Córdoba uses the
commonplace *no des vino a la mujer*, which seems to be
a distortion of Solomon's admonition that kings avoid
women and strong drink.[29]

Woman's lustfulness has led her to adultery, which
she has been known to conceal from her husband in
clever, amusing fashion, often displaying remarkable
ingenuity. In the Hispanic tradition, beginning with the
Disciplina Clericalis of Petrus Alphonsi (born Moisés
Sefardí in Huescas in 1062 and converted to Christianity
in 1106), we find her concealing the flight of her lover
by blinding her husband and mistakenly treating his
good eye when he comes home with a wounded eye
(ex.9); holding up a sheet so that her lover can slip out
of the house (ex.10); pretending her lover is seeking
refuge from street bullies (ex.11); and locking her hus-

band out of his excessively guarded house so that she may remain within with her lover (ex.14).[30] Alfonso Martínez de Toledo uses similar devices, although with a typically original approach characteristic of the irrepressible *arcipreste*—one woman blinds her husband in her apparent desire to impress him with the abundance of the mother's milk she is producing; another holds up a pot which she says needs mending.[31] In the *Libro de los engaños y assayamientos de las mugeres*, translated from the Arabic in 1253, the husband who acted as his wife's procurer dies of chagrin because his wife so obviously enjoys the task of initiating sexually the fat young prince.[32] In all these stories, even though the ostensible moral purpose is to condemn feminine deceitfulness, the man is the comic figure, as is certainly the case with the man who awakens to find himself a tonsured member of a religious order as a result of his wife's deception.[33]

Besides threatening the established order by undermining matrimony, which was the first sacrament (instituted in Eden), woman's lust causes her to provoke lust in otherwise saintly, ascetic men. Sánchez Vercial collected a number of stories in the fifteenth century, in which the woman is an unwitting temptress. Such is the case of the cleric's mother, whose son found it necessary to envelop his hands in his cloak while carrying her across a swollen stream. On the other hand the *mugier pública* who spent the night in a hermit's house in order to tempt him was aware of what she was doing.[34]

The parallel is inescapable—Jewish sexuality, especially the marriage laws of the Jews and the dangers of intermarriage with Jews, threatens Christian matrimony just as feminine sexuality threatens to destroy marriage as such. In addition woman's provocative behavior causes clerical discomfort even when it does not actually threaten to destroy clerical celibacy as an ecclesiastical practice.

The second characteristic attributed to both Jews and women was that they were treacherous, disloyal, and the cause of discord and dissension. We have seen how lust was related to those other intemperate practices of gluttony and drunkenness. In the same way treachery, disloyalty, and divisiveness were related to wiliness in dealing with others and to sharp practices. The unreliability of both Jews and women is clearly and succintly expressed in the proverb: *Judío o mujer que jura, malicia segura.*[35]

Certainly the Jew as the betrayer of God was a medieval commonplace. Titus was said to have burnt the city of Jerusalem not only because the Jews killed Jesus, but also because Titus was disgusted by their contentious, disloyal behavior during the siege.[36] The prophecy of Deuteronomy 21:22–23 was fulfilled and they were never again to have their own kingdom. In the definition of what a Jew is, the *Siete Partidas* explains:

> The Church, emperors, kings, and other princes suffer the Jews to live among Christians so that they might live as if in captivity for ever as a reminder to all men that they came from the lineage of those who crucified our Lord, Jesus Christ. (*Partida* VII, *título* xxiv, *ley* 1, III, 670)

In the *Duelo de la Virgen* Gonzalo de Berco (ca. 1180–1250) deals with the unattractive behavior of the Jews after the crucifixion. The poem (210 *coplas* in *cuaderna vía*) shows the Virgin telling St. Bernard what she has suffered. She tells him how the Jews went to Pilate to warn him that the disciples might try to steal Jesus' body in order to make the prophecy of the resur-

rection appear to have come true (*copla* 166). Pilate
mockingly assigns them to guard duty, calling them
fardidos peones, clearly a mock heroic epithet (*copla*
172); he warns them not to get drunk, nor to leave their
post to visit their wives (*copla* 175). Berceo describes
the Jews as a disorderly group, approaching the tomb
mouthing insults, singing vile songs, and playing musical instruments (*coplas* 176–177). Pilate has already
suggested that they make up some songs, a perfect introduction for the little tune they begin to sing, which,
with the *estribillo* of *eya velar* is an exhortation to vigi-
lance. The Apostles are accused of venality, and the
Jews express their doubt that Jesus will be able to lift
the heavy stone that seals his tomb (*coplas* 178–190).[37]

We find other evidences of the Jew as a traitorous
person in Hispanic literature. Solomon Katz gives a
good summary of the historical sources dealing with the
Jewish participation in the treachery which made possible the Arab invasion of the Iberian peninsula in 711.[38]
Both Rodrigo Ximénez de Rada (1180–1247) in *De
Rebus Hispaniae* and Lucas de Tuy (el Tudense, d.1249)
in his *Chronicon Mundi* mention that the Jews welcomed the invaders. Much later, in the *Sentencia* leveled
against the *conversos* by Pedro Sarmiento in 1449, the
Jews were accused of the terrible treachery of having
handed over the city of Toledo to Tarife, the Arab in-
vader, so that 306 *cristianos viejos* were beheaded and
more than 106 were dragged from church and taken
prisoner. The story was repeated in the fifteenth century
to comment on the fact that the *conversos*, who were
descendants of those early Jews, were still behaving in
the same disloyal, unreliable way.[39] That the Jewish
population had welcomed the Arab invaders and had
betrayed their Christian neighbors was only a part of

their guilt in connection with the events of 711. In a
curious bifurcation of the legend of the last Visigothic
king, whose indiscretion had set off the treachery of
Count Julian, the *Hispano-romanos* of the north of
Spain attributed the guilt to Witiza, a friend of the
Jews, and not to Rodrigo. In the *Primera crónica general* we find the struggle between Egica (687–701),
Witiza (697–701) and Theudofredo, father of Rodrigo
(701–710). Witiza, *enemigo de Dios*, exiled Theudofredo and his son Rodrigo to Córdoba. According to his
enemies, Witiza unfairly gave preference and privi-
leges to the Jews and neglected the Church during his
reign.[40] Witiza was deposed in favor of Rodrigo (the
last Visigoth), and it certainly seems possible that Witiza's adherents, many of whom were Jews, might have
been anxious to end Rodrigo's rule. That Count Julian,
father of La Cava, the immediate cause of the betrayal
(in the legend), was a Jew is mentioned by a modern
scholar, but I find no such identification.[41]

In the *Cántigas de Santa Maria*, written by Alfonso el
Sabio, it is said that devotion to the Virgin had been cast
out of Spain because of the actions of the Jews and the
heretics.[42] More to the point, in *Cántiga* 348 a king,
possibly Alfonso himself, asks the Virgin for help in
finding money to continue the holy fight against the
Moors. She tells him where to find great treasure buried
by the Jews. The suggestion is clear—the Jews would
not be loyal to the throne, nor would they help with the
Reconquest unless forced to do so.[43]

Feminine treachery is described in similar terms. Obviously much patristic literature credits Eve with the
expulsion from Paradise, as does much misogynistic
prose. Her culpability was, in fact, the same kind of
commonplace as was Jewish responsibility for the cruci-

fixion. Similarly, just as Jews were set apart as treacherous and unreliable in the *Siete Partidas*, so were women. Ruth Lansing writes:

> The feeling that woman is unreliable prevails—
> she is evidently a dangerous and tricky character.
> The third *Partida* particularly shows a tendency to
> class her with the physically defective and the
> morally irresponsible.[44]

Women, or more specifically a woman, La Cava, shared the responsibility with the Jews for the Moorish invasion. The traditional story of Rodrigo and his lust for La Cava, daughter of Count Julian, is told as a sort of politically etiological tale to explain why the Arabs found it so easy to invade Spain.[45] The constant in the tale is that this attractive young woman had no more business bathing where the king could see her and be inflamed by her beauty and by her nakedness than had had Bathsheba to bathe and thus to tempt King David. One ballad says she claims she was forced, while Rodrigo says she consented, but subsequent opinion was divided depending on whether a man or a woman were commenting.[46] The *Primera crónica general* shows less interest in assigning the blame, but we do find the comment that Spain was destroyed because of Julian's treachery.[47]

The widowed Lombardian duchess Rosinalda, appears in a Spanish *exemplum* as a woman whose uncontrolled lust causes her to betray her realm when Cacavo, a Hungarian king, lays siege to her castle. She surrenders her castle to him in exchange for a promise that he will marry her. He accedes to her terms, but only for one night, after which he turns her over to his lieutenants,

who use her for three days. The king orders that she
be discarded and that she have the final husband she
merits.[48] Her daughters represent womanly virtue in the
story, putting foul-smelling meat under their breasts so
that they will disgust the conquering troops with their
smell, the reward for which is immediate escape and
ultimately brilliant marriages. Thus woman's lustfulness
leads her into treachery.

Following the pattern of the linking or concatenation
of sins, treachery was related to contentiousness and
deceitfulness. Both Jews and women were said to be
contentious, quarrelsome sowers of discord.

Whether or not the quarrelsome behavior of the Jews
during the siege of Jerusalem was a historical fact, what
is important is that the event was used to underline an
unattractive aspect of their character. In the Hispanic
tradition the story is of particular importance because
one of the most important national legends deals with
the noble resolve of the population of Numancia to
choose suicide over surrender when they can no longer
resist Scipio's siege of their city. It is explained that the
Jews never needed loyalty and unity in biblical times,
since the angels fought on their behalf—the seas parted
for them; the earth swallowed up their enemies.[49] In
the *Caballero Cifar* (1300) the Jews are said to have
caused so much trouble (*escándalo y bullicio*) that the
emperor appointed Herod as their king, thereby beginning the end of their kingdom.[50] They are also blamed
for undermining the good advice of princes, advising
them to tax their people excessively, and playing upon
the greed of princes.[51]

Feminine contentiousness is the theme of the *Libro de
los engaños*. It is the wicked favorite wife of the king
who stirs up all the trouble in the court, confusing the

poor foolish king, who almost kills his son because of her. Unlike Phaedra, her need seems to be for political power rather than for the youth's body. Perhaps the most colorful description of the discord that women are inclined to create appears in Alfonso Martínez de Toledo's vivid seriocomic monologues. Woman stirs up the neighborhood with her malicious gossip (pp. 130–32); her envy of women more beautiful than she provokes a splendidly vituperative description of her rival (pp. 136–43).[52] Womanly beauty is a cause of discord. Alfonso Martínez de Toledo cites Petrarch to the effect that the Trojan War would not have taken place if Helen had not been so beautiful.[53] Helen obviously provoked what ensued. Of woman's disloyalty one need only consider the vast amount of folkloric material dealing with the adulteress who outwits her husband.

Also related to treachery and disloyalty is astuteness or wiliness in dealing with others, with the intention of deceiving them. The Jew appears as the wily moneylender in Alfonso el Sabio's *Cántiga* 25; and in Berceo the tale is *Milagro* XXIII, *"La deuda pagada."*[54] In this traditional tale a Christian in straitened circumstances uses the Virgin and her Son as guarantors of a loan. After a miraculous return of the money, the Jew conceals the payment and demands his money.

The story in the Hispanic tradition that offers the most perplexing coincidences is the one that Petrus Alphonsi tells as the *Exemplum de Decem Cofris* (ex. 15). In this story a deceitful woman advises a Spaniard to fill ten coffers with stones to deceive an even more wily Egyptian. Elsewhere Dido, a clever noble woman, fills coffers with sand in order to deceive her evil deceitful brother, Pygmalion, who intends to rob her. In both instances a woman outwits an expert in guile and deception. Boccaccio tells a similar story, observing: "It is a manifest thing that sleights and devices are the more pleasing, the subtler the trickster, who is thereby out-witted" (*Decameron*, 8th day, 10th story). One wonders if there is any special significance in the appearance of the same ruse in the *Poema de Mio Cid*, the national epic, whose more historical episodes take place in eleventh-century Spain. The obviously fictional addition has the ordinarily magnanimous heroic figure Ruy Díaz ordering the preparation of decorated coffers filled with sand to deceive two Jewish moneylenders of Burgus, Raquel and Vidas (lines 85–210). It is possible that the episode is intercalated in the relatively historical narration to emphasize how low the royal exile had brought the *Cid*, but it also represents the out-Jewing of the Jew (deceiving the deceiver) in keeping with the general outline of the traditional folk tale. That the story is generally incompatible with the Hispanic epic tradition seems to be suggested by the ambiguous inclusion of a later scene in which Raquel and Vidas ask for even partial repayment of their loan, which a vassal of Ruy Díaz assures them they will receive (lines 1431–38).[55] The *Primera crónica general* puts a better face on Ruy Díaz's sharp dealings, mentioning a generous repayment and an apology, which the two Jews accept joyfully.[56] The curious juxtaposition of Jews and women and financial deceit, the same tricks being played, should not be used to suggest that Raquel was a woman or that they were a married couple. One can conclude, however, that all these separate elements were related in the popular tradition in a sort of folkloric contamination.

Having seen a similarity in literary attitudes toward Jews and women as sexually overactive creatures and as treacherous, disloyal sowers of discord, we can proceed to the third and final stereotype applied to the two groups. In Christian polemics we find the two groups frequently designated as allies of the Devil. This demonic alliance gave rise to some of the most colorful aspects of what I consider to be serious antifeminism, as opposed to the somewhat frivolous material about lust and deceit which was often a part of folk humor.[57] Demonism was seldom a laughing matter. Related to satanic behavior are the tales of infant sacrifice for religious or culinary reasons, and of course witchcraft.

It is not difficult to establish the connection between the Devil and the Jews and the Devil and women. Joshua Trachtenberg discusses the horned Jew in medieval iconography in relationship to the goat as a symbol of demonic lechery, making the connection with sexuality. Léon Poliakov makes a clear connection when he describes the Devil in sexual terms and calls attention to all of his attributes as "symbols of lewdness and extreme virility." He goes on to describe the link which connects Satan, the witch, the woman, and the Jew, finally pointing out that Jews were thought to have been born misshapen: "They are hemorrhoidal and men as well as women [are] afflicted with menses."[58] The connection between the Jew and the woman is also found in an early thirteenth-century text of a dispute between a Christian and a Jew, in which the Spanish polemicist suggests that the rabbi drinks the blood of the newly circumcized child, contrary to the biblical injunction against the drinking of blood. He goes on:

> Ond, quando bjen uos mesuraredes, fonta uos i iaze & muy grand; que la boca de uestro rabi que conpieça uestra oración, feches cono de muier; & de mas sabedes que la barba y las narizes an y mal

logar. E de mas ueedes qual fonta de sugar sangre
de tal logar. Ond si iusticia fuesse de tierra, mas
derecho era apedrear tal omne que osso ni leon.[59]

In this nasty passage we see a mixture of depravity, per-
version, a hint of magic transformation, and a suggestion of vileness as a part of a religious ritual. As is the
case with deceit and treachery and astuteness, we see a
blurring of the identity of the Jew and the woman when
we consider demonism.

The Jew as a practicer of magic is found in thirteenth-
century peninsular literature. In the *Milagro de Teófilo*
Berceo describes him as follows: he is full of evil vices;
he knows evil enchantments and other artifices; he
makes evil circles and Beelzebub is his teacher and
guide. He is the vassal of Satan who helps him to have
a successful career as a soothsayer so that foolish people
rely on his predictions.[60] In the *Siete Partidas* soothsay-
ers and fortunetellers are condemned in the *título* immediately preceding the section dealing with the Jews. In
fact in the definition of what is a Jew a comparison is
made between fortunetellers who deprecate God by presuming to make themselves His equal (cf. Satan) and
Jews who deny God by not accepting His Son.[61] In another of Berceo's miracles a heavenly voice tells the
Christian worshipers assembled in church on the Feast
of the Assumption that the Jews are mistreating Christ
worse than they ever had before. The entire congrega-
tion run to the house of the chief rabbi and find him
with a large wax figure of Christ crucified.[62] Not only
were Jews magicians, but apparently their religious
leaders were in league with Satan. In the *Siete Partidas*
Alfonso's codifiers of the law showed caution, present-
ing the allegation of Jewish witchcraft as hearsay:

> And because we hear it said that in some places,
> Jews memorialize the passion of Jesus Christ on
> Good Friday stealing children and putting them on
> the Cross or making wax images and crucifying
> them when children are not available. . . .

It was ordered that if these practices could be proved to
have taken place, the offenders would be killed *aviltada-
mente* (which can be rendered as "imaginatively").[63]

From the Church's viewpoint woman and the Devil
were clearly linked. At the same time that it was necessary to advocate clerical celibacy and to condemn women
for tempting holy men, it was also necessary to avoid
the heresy of Tatian, who condemned all matrimony.
One way to relieve women of total responsibility was to
describe them as tools of the Devil and therefore not
inherently evil. Nevertheless they were guilty by association. Fray Martín de Córdoba in the fifteenth century
relies on Ambrose's *Concerning Repentance* to explain
God's choice of the rib as the material for the creation
of Eve, so that she will be Satan's bow in his hunt for
men's souls. Woman is described in the same way by
Luis de Lucena in his *Repetición de amores* and by Fernando de Rojas in the *Celestina*.[64] In all of these instances her sexuality is the connection she has with the
Devil, though she is frequently an innocent tool in his
hands. Martínez-Kleiser reports twenty proverbs directly linking woman and the devil (43.696–43.716).[65]

Fernando de Rojas's Celestina is said to have six
trades: seamstress, perfumer, cosmetic maker, restorer
of maidenheads, go-between, and part-time witch.[66] She
recalls fondly to Pármeno the talents of his mother, who
has been her associate. The departed assiduously visited
cemeteries in order to dig up the remains in search of
the "raw materials of her profession" and once with a

tweezers pulled seven teeth from a hanged man while Celestina was removing his shoes. Celestina says: "And she could enter a witches' circle so much better than I. . . . You can judge her accomplishments when I tell you that the very devils were afraid of her."[67] The two women were arrested four times, one of which was for digging up the earth at a crossroads, a sure sign of witchcraft.[68] Earlier a witch in the *Laberinto* of Juan de Mena had been equipped with the materials from Lucan's *Pharsalia*,[69] clearly a description based on the classical tradition, while Celestina and her colleague were true Hispanic witches.[70] Although the go-between in the weeping bitch story of the *Disciplina Clericalis* does not actually practice any magic, she certainly frightens the young woman with the story of the disappointed lover who has been magically turned into a dog. She turns up in the *Libro de los engaños* and also in Sánchez Vercial.[71]

Continuing the connection with Satan, we know that his sin was pride, presuming to be God's equal, presuming to be a creator in competition with God. Feminine *soberbia* and Jewish *soberbia* can be considered characteristics also linked with the Devil. An intriguing instance of the linking of the two groups is found in the *Arcipreste de Talavera*. In a condemnation of feminine haughtiness and arrogance a woman is quoted daring a man to hit her, because if he does, everyone will talk, since neither toward women, nor Jews, nor clerics ought a man to show defiance or force.[72] He continues to discuss her pride, saying that because of her weak intellect, she believes herself to be equal in knowledge and power with God, as had Lucifer. This error leads her into "committing that which was forbidden," a reference to Eve's error.[73]

Jewish arrogance is a commonplace that stems, perhaps, in part from St. John Chrysostom's characterization of the Jews as a stiff-necked people because they resist the revealed truth. There is an interesting story of a Jew who slips into the church where the Cid's body has lain in state for ten years in a miraculous state of preservation. He is alone with the hero's corpse; everyone else is outside listening to the sermon. He tries to touch Ruy Díaz's beard, an outrage the epic hero would never permit, not even after death. The corpse lifts its sword and frightens the sacrilegious Jew away.[74] The Jew is obviously the outsider, the aloof alien who ignores the established frame of reference of all the rest of the community. The others are listening to the sermon; they certainly would never try to touch the hero's beard, a clear violation of the community's rules. In *Cántiga* 6, a Jew kills and buries a youth who has achieved local fame for his rendition of *Gaude Virgo Maria*; the populace avenges the crime by killing all the Jews in the town and burning the culprit. The Jew's crime was double in that he had not only committed murder, but he had also directed his attack at the Virgin through his victim.[75] The more usual form of the commonplace of Jewish arrogance is found in *Cántiga* 4, and in Berceo's *Milagro* XVI, *"El niño judío,"* an episode which is said to have taken place in France. A young Jewish boy comes home late for dinner and admits to his father, a *can traidor*, *un locco preccador*, and *un falso descreído*, that he has gone to mass and has taken communion (360). The father, also called a *falsso desleal*, chides the lad by putting him into a blazing furnace (361–62). In the *Cántiga* the father is identified as *un judeu . . . que fazer sabía vidrio* and the accompanying miniature shows the furnace to be a glassblower's furnace, assuredly a very hot one.[76] Without doubt the father has displayed his unwillingness to recognize any god but his own; he is stiff-necked indeed.

The bestial behavior of the father calls to mind the persistent accusation of child sacrifice, frequently associated with the practice of witchcraft, but sometimes just evidence of depravity or of subhuman status. Women, too, are capable of horrible acts. Just as antifeminism and antisemitism are blended in the Hispanic tales of deceitfulness, so we find a blurring of the two identities in the story of a Jewish woman suffering the privations and hunger caused by Titus's siege of Jerusalem. Unable to produce mother's milk for her young son, she kills him, roasts him, and eats him. Others smell the roasting meat; she offers them choice parts, a leg and a hand, and then addressing herself directly to her departed child, she says: "Never were you more sweet to me, my son." [77] Was she more Jew or woman in this story? In either case an unnatural, less-than-human creature is here described, as was the case of the Jewish father who put his son in the glass-melting furnace to punish him. These are people who are clearly separate from and outside of the main current of peninsular life.

Recognizing that Jews and women were removed from the shared values of the community to an extent and that both groups were resoundingly condemned insofar as they endangered the Faith, we can offer a few tentative conclusions. In the medieval Hispanic tradition, particularly in didactic literature, both Jews and women were considered to be enemies of the Faith. The Jews challenged the established order by virtue of their very existence, their survival, and even more by their sporadic periods of prosperity and power. Surely people who willfully denied the most important basic truths and who were not destroyed by the divine power they denied must have at the very least represented a perplexity which needed explanation and even justification. In part the justification and explanation were achieved by attributing to the offending group the faults which have been described in this essay.

Women threatened the moral ethical structure in much the same way, merely by their existence. On the one hand they were the source of temptation, an occasion for sin for the otherwise resolute celibates, but on the other hand it was theologically unsound to condemn all matrimony because of the inevitable connection with women it entailed. The apparent solution was to ascribe the guilt to Satan by suggesting that women were his tools as he sought to destroy men. This stance could only lead to the disquieting feeling that there was something apart, alien, and wrong about women, just as there was about Jews, thereby creating the "justifiable and respectable reason" for prejudice. Perhaps, ultimately, the only conclusion to be drawn is that both Jews and women were each in their own way outsiders in the Hispanic literary tradition. Their having been singled out as excessively sexual creatures, as treacherous disloyal citizens, and as Satanic companions dealing in witchcraft, arrogant Satanic pride, and all kinds of depravity was merely a way of assigning to the outcasts of society all the sins the community feared most.

NOTES

1. Isidore Epstein, *The "Responsa" of Rabbi Solomon Ben Adreth of Barcelona* (1235–1310) (1925; rpt. New York, 1968), p. 1.
2. Arthur Lukyn Williams, *Adversus Judaeos: A*

Bird's-Eye View of Christian Apologiae until the Renaissance (Cambridge, 1935), p. 207.

3. Kenneth R. Scholberg, "Minorities in Medieval Castilian Literature," *Hispania* 37(1954–55): 204 and 208 n. 6.

4. Fernando Rubio Álvarez, "Desfavorable concepto moral de la mujer en algunas obras de origen oriental," *Ciudad de Dios* 177(1964): 286.

5. See Barbara Matulka, *An Antifeminist Treatise of XVth Century Spain: La repetición de amores* (New York, 1931); María Pilar del Oñate, *El femenismo en la literatura española* (Madrid, 1938); Jacob Ornstein, "La misoginia y el profemenismo en la literatura castellana," *Revista de filología hispánica* 3(1941): 219–32; Luis de Lucena, *Repetición de amores*, ed. Jacob Ornstein (Chapel Hill, 1954); Fray Martín de Córdoba, *Jardín de nobles donzellas: A Critical Edition and Study*, ed. Harriet Goldberg, *University of North Carolina Studies in the Romance Languages and Literatures* 137 (Chapel Hill, 1974).

6. It is clear that by the fifteenth century antifeminism had become part of the games that poets and courtiers played. Fernando Rubio Álvarez points out that even the most celebrated *Maldezir de las mujeres* by Pedro Torellas ended with a palinode directed to his lady: "Vos sois la que deshacéis/ lo que contienen mis versos," ('You are she who gives the lie to my verses') so that the courtly debate was not related to serious misogyny (p. 272).

7. See Adolfo de Castro, *The History of the Jews in Spain*, tr. Edward D.G.M. Kirwan (London, 1851); José Amador de los Ríos, *Historia social y política de los judíos de España* 3 vols. (Madrid,

1875–1876); Solomon Katz, *The Jews in the Visigothic and Frankish Kingdoms of Spain and Gaul* (1937; rpt. New York, 1970); Yitzhak Baer, *A History of the Jews in Christian Spain* 2 vols., tr. Louis Schoffman (Philadelphia, 1966); Abraham Neuman, *The Jews in Spain* 2 vols. (Philadelphia, 1942), James Parkes, *The Conflict of the Church and the Synagogue: A Study in the Origins of Antisemitism* (New York, 1964); Léon Poliakov, *A History of Antisemitism*, tr. Richard Howard (New York, 1965); Marcel Simon, *Verus Israel* (Paris, 1964); Stephen Gilman, *The Spain of Fernando de Rojas: The Intellectual and Social Landscape of "La Celestina"* (Princeton, 1972); Bernard S. Bachrach, "A Reassessment of Visigothic Jewish Policy, 589-711," *American Historical Review* 78 (1973): 11–34.

8. James Parkes, *Antisemitism* (Chicago, 1964), p. 12.

9. See Stith Thompson, *Motif-Index of Folklore Literature* 6 vols. (Bloomington, Indiana, 1955–1958) and John Esten Keller, *Motif-Index of Medieval Spanish Exempla* (Knoxville, 1949), T330–360. Keller includes more than twenty-five variants in his index.

10. St. Jerome, *The Principal Works of St. Jerome*, tr. W.H. Fremantle, G. Lewis, and W.G. Martley, *A Select Library of the Nicene and Post-Nicene Fathers of the Christian Church*, 2nd Series (New York, 1893), p. 378.

11. St. Ambrose, *Concerning Repentance* in *Some Principal Works of St. Ambrose*, tr. H. Romestin and E.D. Romestin, *A Select Library . . .* 2nd Series (1880; rpt. Grand Rapids, Michigan, 1955) Bk. I, Ch. xiv, pp. 340–41.

12. St. Augustine, *The City of God*, Vol. II: Bks. VIII–XXII, tr. Gerald G. Walsh and Grace Monahan, *The Fathers of the Church*, 3 vols. (New York, 1954), II, 274, Bk. XII, Ch. xvi.

13. James Parkes, *The Conflict of the Church and the Synagogue*, p. 375.

14. Alfonso el Sabio, *Primera crónica general de España que mandó componer Alfonso el Sabio y se continuaba bajo Sancho IV en 1289 publicada por Ramón Menéndez Pidal*, ed. Antonio G. Solalinde, Manuel Muñoz Cortés and José Gómez Pérez, 2 vols. (Madrid, 1955), I, p. 136.

15. See Goldberg, *Jardín de nobles donzellas*, pp. 121–23 for an application of Henri Bergson's definition of the risible to these *exempla*.

16. Marcel Simon, *Verus Israel*, p. 245. See also Acts 7:51–52 in which Jews are described as: "Stiffnecked and uncircumcised in your heart and ears, ye do always resist the Holy Ghost; as your fathers did, so did ye."

17. Alfonso Martínez de Toledo, *Arcipreste de Talavera o corbacho*, ed. J. González Muela (Madrid, 1970), p. 146. The *Arcipreste* describes woman as a two-faced creature in Part II, ch. 5.

18. See *A Catholic Commentary*, ed. Dom Bernard Orchard et al. (New York, 1953), 514j. In 456g it is noted that God is often spoken of as the spouse of Israel.

19. St. John Chrysostom, *Adversus Judaeos, Patrologia Graeca* 48, 846–53. St. John's enthusiastic style apparently contaminated him. His own reputation suffered, and we find him named as the father of the illegitimate son of the sovereign's daughter, for which he was exiled. In exile the holy man ran out of ink and dipped his pen in his own saliva,

which turned into golden letters on the page, earning him the name *Juan Boca de Oro* (Clemente Sánchez Vercial, *El libro de los exenplos a.b.c.*, ed. John Esten Keller [Madrid, 1961], p. 221). The concatenation of lust and gluttony and drunkenness was referred to by St. Jerome, who quoted Terence: "When Ceres fails, and Liber, Venus droops" (St. Jerome, *Letter LIV*, p. 105). Fray Martín de Córdoba picks up the same quotation: "Dize Terencio que sin Ceres, ques la diosa del pan, sin Baco, ques el dios del vino, enfríase Venus ques la diosa de amores carnales" (p. 277).

20. *The Works now extant of St. Justin the Martyr*, tr. G.J. Davie (Oxford, 1861), p. 235.

21. I. Epstein, *The "Responsa,"* p. 88.

22. Fray Martín de Córdoba, p. 376.

23. Eloy Benito Ruano, "El memorial contra los conversos del bachiller Marcos García de Mora (Marquillos de Mazarambroz)," *Sefarad* 17(1957): 314–51. In the *Memorial* it is said that D. Álvaro de Luna the *condestable* was influenced to perform "grandísimas e intolerables cruelidades e inhumanidades" by the Jews who were "adúlteros fijos de incredulidad e infidelidad, padres de toda cobdicia, sembradores de toda cizaña e diuisión, abundados en toda malicia e peruersidad, ingratos siempre a Dios, contrarios a sus mandamientos" (p. 321) ("adulterous sons of disbelief and faithlessness, fathers of all covetousness, sowers of all discord and dissension, abounding with all kinds of malice and perversity, eternally ungrateful to God, and to His commandments").

24. *Las Siete Partidas del rey don Alfonso el Sabio*, ed. Real Academia de la Historia, 3 vols. (Madrid, 1972).

25. Woman as a physically damaging being is described by Norman Penzer, *Poison-Damsels and other essays in Folklore and Anthropology* (London, 1952). In these stories the sweat glands of a woman are thought to give off a contact poison. She appears thus in the Pseudo-Aristotle's advice to Alexander, translated into Castilian in the thirteenth century as *Poridat de las poridades* (ed. Lloyd Kasten [Madrid, 1957], p. 41).

26. Hermann Knust, *Mittheilungen aus dem Eskurial* (Tübingen, 1879), p. 503.

27. Fray Martín de Córdoba, p. 195. See also Luis de Lucena, p. 85.

28. *Arcipreste de Talavera*, "hot with wine or aroused," p. 167.

29. Fray Martín de Córdoba, "Don't give wine to a woman." See Proverbs 31:3–5: "Give not thy strength unto women, nor thy ways to that which destroyeth kings. It is not for kings to drink wine; nor for princes strong drink. Lest they drink and forget the law, and pervert the judgment of any of the afflicted."

30. Petrus Alphonsi, *Disciplina Clericalis*, ed. Ángel González Palencia (Madrid, 1948). Although Jacob Ornstein denies that translated works such as the *Disciplina Clericalis* and the *Libro de los engaños* were Hispanic works (*Repetición de amores*, p. 14), it is my opinion that their having been translated in Spain, by Spaniards, for the use of Spanish readers makes them a part of the Hispanic literary tradition.

31. Arcipreste de Talavera, pp. 162–65.

32. *El libro de los engaños y assayamientos de las mugeres*, ed. John Esten Keller (Chapel Hill, 1959), pp. 27–28.

33. Sánchez Vercial, *El libro des los exenplos*, p. 240.

34. *Ibid.*, p. 196.

35. Luis Martínez-Kleiser, *Refranero general ideológico español* (Madrid, 1953), 34.710. "A Jew or a woman who makes a vow, is certain malice."

36. *Primera crónica general*, I, p. 133 and I, p. 101.

37. Gonzalo de Berceo, *Duelo de la Virgen* in *BAE* 57 (Madrid, 1864), *Poetas castellanos anteriores al siglo XV*, ed. Florencio Janer, pp. 131–137. *In the Poema de mío Cid*, the heroic epithet *ardida lanza* refers to knights, not foot soldiers.

38. S. Katz, *The Jews in the Visigothic and Frankish Kingdoms*, pp. 116–17.

39. Pedro Sarmiento, "Sentencia que Pedro Sarmiento, asistente de Toledo e el Común de la Ciudad Dieron en el año 1449 contra los conversos," in Alfonso de Cartagena, *Defensorium unitatis christianae* (Madrid, 1943), pp. 362–63.

40. *Primera crónica general*, I, p. 306

41. See Albert Bagby, Jr., "The Jews in the *Cántigas* of Alfonso X el Sabio," *Speculum* 46 (1971): 670–88, n. 37. The *Primera crónica general* says: "E el cuende Julián era un grand fidalgo, et uinié de grand linnage de partes de los godos" (I,307). Ramón Menéndez Pidal reports the first directly Spanish version of the legend in a *Chronica gothorum Pseudo-Isidoriana* written in the first half of the eleventh century. In this version, the story belongs to the *gageure* cycle, beginning with a wager made in front of Witiza that the daughter of Count Julian of Tangitania was the most beautiful woman in the world (*Floresta de leyendas heróicas españolas*, 3 vols. [Madrid, 1925], I, 28–30).

42. Alfonso X el Sabio, *Cántigas de Santa María*, ed. Walter Mettman, 3 vols. (Coimbra, 1959–1964),

I, 7, *Cántiga* 2, 20–25. This is a poetic reference to Jewish cooperation with the invading Arabs.

43. *Cántigas*, III, 242–243. *Cántiga* 348, tells of the treasure: "jaz so terra, que meteron y mui peyores ca mouros" (v. 28) "it lies beneath the earth, people worse than the Moors put it there." The owners of the treasure are identified: "dos judeos, seus ẽemigos, a que quer peor ca mouros" (49), "of the Jews, her enemies, who are worse than the Moors."

44. Ruth Lansing, "The Thirteenth Century Legal Attitude Toward Woman in Spain," *Publications of the Modern Language Association* 36 (1921): 507.

45. Ramón Menéndez Pidal, *Romancero tradicional. Romanceros del rey Rodrigo y de Bernardo del Carpio*, ed. Diego Catalán Mz. Pidal, Rafael Lapesa, A. Galmés and J. Caso (Madrid, 1957) I, 4–7. Those who blamed Witiza might have been further angered at him because of his preferential treatment of the Jews in his realm.

46. *Romancero tradicional*, p. 109. The lines are: "Si dicen quién de los dos / la mayor culpa ha tenido, / digan los hombres: La Cava, / y las mujeres: Rodrigo." Colin C. Smith notes that the novelization of the story by Pedro del Corral in his *Crónica Sarracina* (in Floresta . . . I, 178–287) was called a *trufa o mentira paladina* "hoax and a flagrant lie," in 1455 by Hernán Pérez de Guzmán (*Spanish Ballads* [London: Pergamon Press, 1969], p. 51). La Cava is said to be derived from the Arabic *alacaba* "whore."

47. *Primera crónica general*, I, p. 308.

48. Sánchez Vercial, *El libro de los exenplos*, p. 192. Cacavo revealed himself to be a serious misogynist:

"E al tercero día fízoles poner un palo por la na-
tura fasta la garganta, deziendo:—Tal mugier
luxuriosa que por cobdicia de luxuria de su carne
perdió su cibdat, e tal marido conviene aver;"
"And on the third day he ordered them to put a
rod through her parts up to her throat, saying:—
Such a lustful woman who because of her lustful
carnal desires lost her city, deserves to have such a
husband."

49. *Primera crónica general*, I, p. 133.
50. *El libro del cauallero Zifar*, ed. Charles Philip
    Wagner (Ann Arbor, 1929), p. 332.
51. *Zifar*, p. 330.
52. *Arcipreste de Talavera*, pp. 136–43. Cf. the same
    kind of tirade in *La Celestina* in which the two
    whores, Elicia and Areusa, make unflattering
    remarks about Melibea's beauty (Fernando de
    Rojas, *La Celestina*, ed. Julio Cejador y Frauca, 2
    vols. [Madrid, 1965], II, pp. 31–34).
53. *Arcipreste de Talavera*, pp. 140–41.
54. Gonzalo de Berceo, *Milagros de Nuestra Señora*,
    ed. Antonio G. Solalinde (Madrid, 1964), *coplas*
    625–700, pp. 146–61.
55. *El Poema de mio Cid*, ed. Ramón Menéndez Pidal
    (Madrid, 1960).
56. *Primera crónica general*, I, pp. 593–94. See also
    Colin Smith, ed. *Poema de mío Cid* (Oxford,
    1972), p. 127 for Smith's observation that the
    "merry anti-Semitism" of the thirteenth century
    had changed so that in the fourteenth-century
    chronicle the explanation was needed. Edmund de
    Chasca, ("Toward a Redefinition of Epic Formula
    in the Light of the *Cantar de Mio Cid*," *Hispanic
    Review* 38 [1970]: 263) sees the episode as "high-

ly amusing to all," citing also Dámaso Alonso's opinion that the *juglar* used the trick to "delight his audience with the tonic of laughter." Cesáreo Bandera Gómez (*"El Poema de Mío Cio": poesía, historia, mito* [Madrid, 1969], p. 118) remarks that the *Cid* deceives Raquel and Vidas using their own covetousness against them. J. Rodríguez-Puértolas ("El realismo del *Poema de Mío Cid*," *Publications of the Modern Language Association* 82 [1967]: 172, n. 21) sees irony in the tale and not antisemitism "strictu senso."

57. One might venture the opinion that many of the exempla ostensibly critical of feminine lust and deceitfulness are really antimasculine in that the man is the object of ridicule. See Goldberg, ed. *Jardín de nobles donzellas*, pp. 121–23. A similar inversion of normal values, in a Bergsonian sense, might lie behind the humor in the Raquel and Vidas episode.

58. Poliakov, *History of Antisemitism*, pp. 141–43; Joshua Trachtenberg, *The Devil and the Jews; The Medieval Conception of the Jew and Its Relation to Modern Antisemitism* (New Haven, 1943), pp. 44–47. He also notes the incidence of male menstruation and hemorrhoids (p. 50).

59. Américo Castro, "Disputa entre un cristiano y un judío," *Revista de filología española* 1(1914): 176; "Whereas when you think well upon it [you will see that] you commit an outrageous act that lies herein; that the mouth of your rabbi who begins your prayers, you make it into a woman's cunt; and even more you know that the chin and the nose don't belong there. And even more you see what an outrage it is to suck blood from such

a place. Whereas if there were justice in the earth it would be more just to stone such a man than to stone a bear or a lion."

60. Berceo, *Milagros, coplas* 722–26, pp. 165–66.

61. *Siete Partidas, Partida* VII, *título* xxiii, *ley* I, III, 667.

62. Berceo, *Milagros, coplas* 413–60, pp. 101–10.

63. *Siete Partidas, Partida* VII, *título* xxiv, *ley* 2.

64. Martín de Córdoba, p. 154; Luis de Lucena, p. 67; *La Celestina*, I, 49–50.

65. *Refranero general ideológico* . . .

66. *La Celestina*, I, pp. 69–86. Her paraphernalia included the rope used to hang a man, cauls, and other usual magic objects. She was said to paint magic saffron-colored letters in the palm of a hand and to give to some wax hearts stuck with broken needles and things made of lead "too frightful to describe." See also Alfonso Martínez de Toledo's description of these women, *Arcipreste de Talavera*, p. 172.

67. *La Celestina*, I, pp. 238–44.

68. John T. McNeill and Helen M. Gamer (*Medieval Handbook of Penance* [New York, 1938], p. 334) mention the custom of erecting crosses at crossroads at which offerings were left. They also say that crossroads were often the scene of strange worship.

69. Juan de Mena, *El laberinto de la fortuna*, ed. José Manuel Blecua (Madrid, 1968), *coplas* 241–43.

70. For a description of a Hispanic witch who also was incidentally Jewish, see Stephen Gilman, cited in n. 7.

71. *Disciplina Clericalis*, Ex. 13; *Libro de los engaños*, pp. 29–31; Sánchez Vercial, *El libro de los exenplos*, pp. 235–36.

72. *Arcipreste de Talavera*, p. 156.
73. *Ibid.*, p. 159.
74. *Primera crónica general*, I, pp. 642–43.
75. *Cántigas*, I, 21–23.
76. Berceo, Milagros, *coplas* 352–77, pp. 88–93; *Cántigas*, I, pp. 10–14.
77. *Primera crónica general*, I, p. 135. The same story is told without the remarkable dialogue in the *Castigos e documentos del rey don Sancho*, (ed. Gayangos, *BAE*, 51, Cap. 5, p. 96a). In this didactic work attributed to Sancho IV el Bravo, the son of Alfonso el Sabio, she is more clearly woman than Jew: "E non se puede fallar que padre por cuita que hobiese nunca comiese fijo, como esta mujer que comió el suyo;" "And one can't find a father who because of distress would eat his son as this woman ate hers."

MEDIEVAL JEWISH IMAGE: CONTROVERSIES, CONTRIBUTIONS, CONCEPTIONS

Joseph Gutmann

Heinrich Graetz, a German Jewish historian, wrote in 1846 that ". . . paganism sees its God, Judaism hears him."[1] This statement has been echoed and reechoed many times. Martin Buber says: "The Jew of antiquity was more of an aural than a visual being and felt more in terms of time than space," while even Bernard Berenson claims that Jews displayed no talent for the figurative arts: "To the Jews belonged the splendours and the raptures of the word."[2] Even today prevailing scholarly opinion still holds that Judaism, hampered by an all-embracing biblical injunction—the Second Commandment—always denied the Image. However such a conclusion can be reached only if one assumes that the Second Commandment is an unchanging concept in a static Jewish culture. It overlooks the fact that a dynamic Judaism, over its three-thousand-year history, spawned many diverse types of Judaism, each with a different interpretation of the Second Commandment. On the one hand Profiat Duran, a fifteenth-century Spanish Jew, wrote:

> The contemplation and study of pleasing forms,
> beautiful images, and drawings broadens and stim-
> ulates the mind and strengthens its faculties. . . .
> As with God, who wanted to beautify His Holy
> Place with gold, silver, jewels, and precious stones,
> so it should be with His holy books.[3]

On the other hand in Germany, in that same century,
Rabbi Jacob Mölln strenuously objected to using beauti-
fully decorated prayerbooks for religious services.[4]

Furthermore the theory that Judaism always denied
the image does not take into consideration the fact that
there is frequently a wide divergence between dogmatic
verbalizations of religious leaders of a particular society
and the practices actually adhered to by large segments
of its population. This holds true for Christianity as
well as for Judaism. St. Bernard in twelfth-century
Clairvaux stated: "For God's sake, if men are not
ashamed of these follies [ridiculous monsters sculpted
in the cloisters], why at least do they not shrink from
the expense?"[5] Rabbi Meir of thirteenth-century Rothen-
burg wrote: "It does not seem fitting to me, since when
they [the readers] contemplate these figures [animal
and bird figures in prayer books] they will not incline
their hearts to their Father in heaven."[6] We know how
little St. Bernard's strictures were heeded, and we will
see that Rabbi Meir's pronouncements were equally
ignored.

In a few scholarly circles the pendulum has recently
swung to the other extreme. From outright denial of
the existence of the Jewish image, some scholars are
now convinced that the ultimate source of many Old
Testament scenes in early and medieval Christian art
was a flourishing Jewish art. "No other explanation can
account for the existence of different Jewish elements in

Christian art in various places and styles," asserts one scholar.[7] In support of this theory scholars cite the amazing third-century Dura-Europos synagogue. Its cycle of paintings, it is claimed, is based on illustrated manuscript cycles, iconographic traces of which survive in later Christian and Jewish manuscripts. One unusual iconographic motif from the Dura synagogue (fig. 1) that seems to have survived for a thousand years to re-appear in fourteenth-century Spanish Hebrew manu-scripts (fig. 2) has been used to demonstrate the exis-tence of Jewish manuscript cycles. It shows the naked Egyptian princess discovering the child Moses in the Nile River. The immediate model of the Spanish He-brew miniature, however, is not the Dura painting, but perhaps a late-twelfth-century Pamplona Bible (fig. 3). The artistic and literary sources for this unusual motif, as well as others in the Pamplona Bibles, have yet to be explored.[8]

In general the assumption of manuscript sources for the Dura paintings cannot be substantiated. Recent re-search indicates that the Dura paintings are probably based on pattern or model books. Furthermore no illus-trated Jewish manuscripts are known from antiquity; the earliest extant date only from the late ninth century. Unlike manuscript cycles, the biblical paintings at Dura (fig. 4) do not follow a narrative sequential order and are not placed on the walls to enrich and explain the stories of the Bible; rather they are themes purposely chosen from many books of the Bible and extrabiblical literature in order to spell out, in an analogous fashion, a definite theological program of contemporary Juda-ism.[9]

Scholars also assume that the appearance of supple-mentary figures often depicted in Christian miniatures stems from lost Jewish manuscript sources. Until recently these figures were dismissed as novelistic embellishments attributable to figments of the artists' imagination, but it has been demonstrated that they can be attributed to *aggadah*—the vast body of Jewish homiletical and legendary literature, whose texts magnify, clarify, and amplify the basic biblical text. A clear example is in the sixth-century Vienna Genesis, where the winged angel that Joseph encounters when seeking his brethren has been identified as the angel Gabriel, whereas the Bible simply mentions Joseph's meeting a man. Similarly the naked child in the crib next to Joseph, as he looks back to the scene of temptation with Potiphar's wife, may be the child who gave testimony of Joseph's innocence to Potiphar. The Bible gives no warrant for these scenes, but legends in extrabiblical traditions do.[10] In a twelfth-century Octateuch miniature we find in the Garden of Eden a serpent that has mounted a camel-like creature, thereby giving the appearance of having four legs. In a thirteenth-century mosaic at San Marco the raven sent forth by Noah has not returned to the ark, but is shown instead feasting on a carcass. Again extrabiblical sources provide ready explanations.[11]

There can be little doubt that one of the great contributions of Judaism to Christian art (and, it may be added, to Muslim art as well) is the great storehouse of Jewish legendary lore which was taken over by Christianity and Islam and creatively adapted to suit their own unique traditions. There is no need, therefore, to posit Jewish illustrated manuscript sources for these scenes, since literary sources probably served as adequate channels of transmission and inspiration. Two legendary motifs from the life of Abraham, which appear simultaneously in Christian, Islamic, and Jewish art from the fourteenth century on illustrate this point.

According to Jewish legend, Abraham's search for the one God finally led to his rejection of idol worship. In Queen Mary's Psalter of the early fourteenth century Terah, Abraham's father, is seated at a workbench carving idols in the shape of cows and handing them to Abraham to sell in the market (fig. 5). In another scene Abraham is about to throw one of the carved idols on the ground, while at the same time trampling another idol. Five astonished witnesses watch the deed. The text explaining the miniature reads:

> Here Abram breaks the false gods to pieces in despite, and the men of the law see him and marvel thereat. God keep you, Terah, wherever you may be. Your gods are all broken into pieces. Abram here says to his father, on themselves they have no mercy.[12]

An early-fourteenth-century miniature in *The Chronology of Ancient Nations* of al-Bīrūnī features Abraham, axe in hand, chopping an idol lying on the ground, while two idols sit behind the fallen one as mute witnesses (fig. 6). The text states that Abraham entered an idol temple and "seized by wrath, broke the idols in pieces, and left their company."[13]

A Jewish miniature in a fourteenth-century Spanish Haggadah simply shows the iconoclast striking a crowned idol with a stick, in keeping with Jewish legend (fig. 7).[14]

According to Jewish legendary fancy, Abraham's rash act of iconoclasm was severely punished by King Nimrod, who ordered Abraham to be cast into the fire of the Chaldeans. We find illustrations of this legend in fourteenth-century *Speculum Humanae Salvationis*

manuscripts. Usually Abraham is engulfed by flames
and God reaches down from the arc of Heaven to rescue
him from the flames (fig. 8):

> Behold, God prefigured this liberation of man
> In compassion [the true God] liberated him [Abra-
>   ham] from the fire of the Chaldeans
> And kept Abraham in the fire without being
>   burned.[15]

Persian manuscripts of Rashīd al-Dīns *Collection of
Histories* (Jāmic al-Tāwārīkh) from fourteenth-century
Tabriz also illustrate this legend. Nimrod is surrounded
by his advisers and is seated to the right of a large siege
catapult. According to Muslim tradition, Nimrod had
ordered Abraham to be placed in the center of huge
piles of wood which were to be kindled. The flames
leaped so high no one could approach the fire. Satan
(Eblis) came to the rescue and helped construct a catapult with which to project Abraham into the fire. The
fire, however, became cold, and when Nimrod dared
gaze at the scene, he beheld " a spring gushing forth
from the midst of the fire and around this spring, there
was a flowerbed, with Abraham seated beside the
water," as in our miniature (fig. 9).[16]
  Jewish manuscripts from the fourteenth century also
feature depictions of this legend. In an early-fourteenth-
century Haggadah from Catalonia we note a crowned
Nimrod enthroned under a baldachin, two courtiers at
his feet, while he points towards a kneeling Abraham
whom two servants are pushing into a fiery furnace.
From the flames of the furnace two winged angels extend their arms to receive him (fig. 10). In a south German prayerbook from around 1320 we see the monarch,

to the left, sitting in judgment. On the right, the hand
of God appears to reach from heaven toward the outstretched arms of Abraham to save him from the midst
of the flames.

All the images reveal such a rich diversity of iconography and styles of basic legendary motifs in the three
religions as to refute the claim of a common descent
from lost Jewish manuscript models. They argue very
strongly in favor of artistic inventiveness and original-
ity. There is no doubt, however, that these depictions
are indebted to Jewish legendary lore that Muslim and
Christian scholars freely adapted to suit their own
unique religious traditions.[17]

We have seen that the common cliché about the non-
existence of Jewish art cannot be upheld any more than
the claim of extensive lost illustrated Jewish manuscript
cycles. Jewish legendary lore, creatively adapted by
Christian and Muslim scholars, had a great impact on
and made a significant contribution to the art of these
religions.

A Jewish iconography that was distinct from Christian iconography did develop and flourish during the
Middle Ages. This iconography reveals no unique Jewish style, as Jews adapted the dominant styles of their
Christian environment.[18] Two examples should suffice to
make this clear. The Sacrifice of Isaac in two early-
thirteenth-century German works of art reveal how
closely the Jewish miniature is patterned after its Christian model (figs. 11–12). Unlike earlier Jewish art, the
Dura synagogue for instance, no hand of God appears
to intervene, nor is the ram tied or standing next to a
tree (fig. 13). Instead, as in the Christian example, a
winged angel stops the deed, and the ram is entangled
in the thicket. In accord with thirteenth-century conven-

tions Isaac is sitting nude on top of the faggots on the altar. Spanish Hebrew manuscripts from the early fourteenth century again follow Christian models. The gold diapered background, the division of the page into four framed panels, and the slender, graceful figures are typical of Gothic art.[19]

Though intricately linked with Christian art in the free use of the dominant contemporary styles, the Jews adapted these styles to express unique Jewish concerns in each country of medieval Europe where they resided. Uppermost in the mind of the medieval Jew was the attainment of salvation in the world to come, and many were the speculations and hopes of what life in the other world might be. We are all familiar with Last Judgment scenes on Gothic tympana, which dramatically spell out the conception of the fate that awaited every Christian in the world to come. Late-thirteenth-early-fourteenth-century Hebrew manuscripts from Germany render a Jewish idea of afterlife. In a thirteenth-century south German Bible we see three primeval beasts on which the righteous dead would feast in the world to come: the *behemoth*, or *shor ba-bar*, represented as a giant steer; the giant fish, known as *livyatan*, Leviathan, rolled up within ocean waves schematically drawn; and the giant bird, known as *ziz* or *bar-yokhani*, depicted as a griffin—a winged quadruped, with its body like a lion and its wings and mask like those of an eagle. In the lower panel five righteous Jews with animal heads and crowns sit at a long table spread with a white cloth and golden vessels. Off to the sides two musicians entertain the righteous dining at the messianic banquet (fig. 14). Although the messianic banquet is a uniquely Jewish expression of the afterlife, the models obviously came from the Bestiaries of the period. Another late-thirteenth-century miniature reveals a ferocious-looking ox, horns lowered, as he makes ready to attack the curled up Leviathan, since God will command Leviathan and Behemoth to engage in mortal combat—"Behemoth will, with its horns, pull Leviathan down and rend it, and Leviathan will, with its fins, pull Behemoth down and pierce it through." [20]

Jewish messianic speculations in Christian Spain during the same period focused not on a messianic banquet, but on the messianic rebuilt Temple in Jerusalem. To emphasize this point the Spanish Jew placed gold and silver implements of the ancient Sanctuary at the beginning of his Bible. We can recognize in a manuscript from Perpignan of 1299 such sacred appurtenances as the golden lampstand, jar of manna, the ark, the altars, lavers, basins, and musical instruments (figs. 15–16). Although many of these vessels are mentioned in the Bible, some are not. The two dishes of frankincense and the three steps next to the lampstand are encountered in Maimonides's twelfth-century legal code, the *Mishneh Torah*. Maimonides scorned naive notions like eternal feasting in the world to come. He did suggest a messianic age in which a Jewish kingdom would be established in the land of Israel under a king-Messiah who would unite Jews into a nation, rebuild the Temple, and reintroduce Jewish law. In keeping with the Jew's daily petition for a speedy restoration of the Temple, our miniature's inscription reads: "May it be Your will that the Temple be speedily rebuilt in our days, so that our eyes may behold it and our heart rejoice."

Furthermore Holy Scripture—the Hebrew Bible—itself came to be called *mikdashyah* ("Sanctuary of God"). Its threefold division (Torah, Prophets, Hagiographa) was likened to the three divisions of the ancient Sanctuary. Hence the Bible was to the Spanish Jew his sanctuary in this world. When it featured illustrations of the ancient Sanctuary vessels on its opening pages, it was merely to give visual expression to his fervent belief in and hope of viewing the restored Temple with its beautiful, sacred implements in the messianic future. The models for some of the vessels seem to have been taken from contemporary Near Eastern ewers and bowls, as we can see in an early-fourteenth-century dragon-spouted ewer (fig. 17).

In fifteenth-century Germany and those parts of northern Italy influenced by German customs, messianic speculations in Hebrew manuscripts no longer centered on the delicacies to be consumed at the messianic banquet as they did in the earlier period. Instead the Jews yearned for the actual coming of the Messiah, who would bring immediate redemption from their unbearable daily miseries. Since Passover was traditionally linked with the night of redemption, the Haggadah, the private liturgical book read at Passover eve was used to express this yearning.

The earliest known miniature of this theme, which is from the second quarter of the fifteenth century, Middle Rhine region, shows a medieval city perched atop a hill next to the Hebrew word *shfoh—pour out* Your wrath upon the nations that do not know You" (Psalm 79:6). From the openings of its towers and houses figures peer out at the scene below. A man, arms outstretched, seems to welcome a crowned figure, blowing a *shofar* and riding upon an ass. This is Elijah, the prophet and the Messiah combined in one person. The streamers in the hands of the figures read: "Say to the daughters of Zion, behold your salvation comes" (Isaiah 62:11) and "Behold your king comes, lowly and riding on an ass"

(Zechariah 9:9). A north Italian manuscript dated 1478 has the head of the house opening the door of his home and holding the prescribed fourth cup of wine in order to recite the *shfoh* to greet the messianic guest. The Messiah is shown as a bearded old man. Seated behind him on the ass are the household of Israel, symbolically riding with the Messiah to the promised redemption (fig. 18).

It should be pointed out that it was customary on Palm Sunday, especially in medieval southern Germany, to have processions where sculpted figures of Christ on his *Palmesel*, or messianic ass, were carried on carts to the gates of a mock Jerusalem (fig. 19). This practice may have exerted some influence on our depictions and caused Jewish leaders to emphasize the traditional Jewish belief that the Messiah was yet to come.

In summary we have tried to demonstrate: 1) that such scholarly controversies as the existence of early Jewish manuscript cycles or the permissibility of art among Jews need reexamination; 2) that Judaism made a considerable contribution to medieval Christian and Islamic art through its vast storehouse of biblical legends; and 3) that Jewish messianic conceptions were unique Jewish artistic expressions of diverse Judaisms in medieval Christian Europe.

NOTES

1. Heinrich Graetz, "Die Construction der jüdischen Geschichte," *Zeitschrift für die religiösen Interessen des Judentums* 3(1846): 86.

2. Martin Buber, *Jüdische Künstler* (Berlin, 1903), p. 7; Bernard Berenson, *Aesthetics and History*

(New York, 1954), p. 180 and cf. Joseph Gutmann, *No Graven Images: Studies in Art and the
Hebrew Bible* (New York, 1971), pp. xiiiff.

3. Isaac ben Moses Duran, *Ma'ase Efod* (Vienna,
1865), p. 19.

4. Jacob ben Moses Mölln, *Sefer Maharil, Hilkhot
Yom Kippur* (Hanau, 1628), fol. 35b.

5. *Patrologia Latina* 182, 915–16.

6. *Tosafot* to Babylonian Talmud, *Yoma* 54a and
Gutmann, p. xix.

7. Bezalel Narkiss, *The Golden Haggadah* (London,
1970), p. 67.

8. Joseph Gutmann, "The Haggadic Motif in Jewish
Iconography," *Eretz-Israel* 6(1960):*17–*18. Cf.
François Bucher, *The Pamplona Bibles* (New
Haven, 1970), pp. 79ff. and 129, n. 15. Cf. also
G. Vermes, "Bible and Midrash: Early Old Testa-
ment Exegesis," *The Cambridge History of the
Bible*, ed. Peter R. Ackroyd and C. F. Evans, I
(Cambridge, 1970), pp. 230–31. Arthur D. Nock,
"The Synagogue Murals of Dura-Europos," *Harry
Austryn Wolfson Jubilee Volume* II (Jerusalem,
1965), pp. 632–33 claims that the Dura scene is
dependent on the Septuagint. This can hardly be
the case, since Byzantine Octateuch miniatures,
which are largely based on the Septuagint, do not
show the nude princess.

9. Cf. the essays by M.L. Thompson, pp. 31–52, B.
Goldman, pp. 53–77 and Joseph Gutmann, pp.
137–54 in Gutmann, ed. *The Dura-Europos Synagogue: A Re-evaluation (1932–1972)*, Religion
and the Arts 1 (Missoula, Mont., 1973).

10. Joseph Gutmann, "Joseph Legends in the Vienna
Genesis," *Proceedings of the Fifth World Congress of Jewish Studies* IV (Jerusalem, 1973), pp.

181–84. Cf. also Élisabeth Revel, "Contribution des textes rabbiniques à l'étude de la Genèse de Vienne," *Byzantion* 42(1972): 115–30 and Suzy Dufrenne, "A propos de deux études récentes sur la Genèse de Vienne," *Byzantion* 42(1972): 598–601 and "Nouvelles remarques sur la Genèse de Vienne," *Byzantion* 43(1973): 504–05.

11. Joseph Gutmann, "Prelude: The Art of the Jews," in *Art and Architecture of Christianity*, ed. Gervis Frere-Cook (Cleveland, 1972), p. 3ff, figs. 12–13. Cf. Gutmann, *No Graven Images*, p. xiff. Cf. also R. Stichel, "Ausserkanonische Elemente in byzantinischen Illustrationen des Alten Testaments," *Römische Quartalschrift* 69(1974): 159ff.

12. George F. Warner, ed. *Queen Mary's Psalter* (London, 1912), p. 58.

13. Edward C. Sachau, ed. and tr., Abu Rayhan Muhammad al-Biruni, *The Chronology of Ancient Nations* (London, 1879), p. 187.

14. Joseph Gutmann, "The Question of Illustrated Jewish Biblical Manuscripts: A Preliminary Investigation," (Rabbinic thesis, Hebrew Union College-Jewish Institute of Religion, Cincinnati, 1957), pp. 20–23,61; and Louis Ginzberg, *The Legends of the Jews* V (Philadelphia, 1947), pp. 217–18.

15. Joseph Gutmann, "Abraham in the Fire of the Chaldeans: A Jewish Legend in Jewish, Christian and Islamic Art," *Frühmittelalterliche Studien* 7 (1973): 347ff.

16. *Ibid.*, p. 348ff.

17. *Ibid.*, p. 345ff.

18. Cf. Joseph Gutmann, "Jewish Art: Fact or Fiction?" *Central Conference of American Rabbis Journal* 12(1964): 49–54.

19. Narkiss, *The Golden Haggadah*, p. 32ff., figs. 1–4.

20. *Leviticus Rabbah* 13.3 and Joseph Gutmann, "When the Kingdom Comes: Messianic Themes in Medieval Jewish Art," *Art Journal* 27(1967–68): figs. 1–6, and "Leviathan, Behemoth and Ziz: Jewish Messianic Symbols in Art," in Gutmann, *No Graven Images*, pp. 515–26. Cf. Jefim Schirmann, "The Battle between Behemoth and Leviathan according to an ancient Hebrew Piyyut," *Proceedings of the Israel Academy of Sciences and Humanities* 4(1970): 327–69.

21. Cf. Gutmann, "Kingdom Comes," pp. 171–73 and Joseph Gutmann "The Messianic Temple in Spanish Medieval Hebrew Manuscripts," in Joseph Gutmann, ed., *The Temple of Solomon: Archaeological Fact and Medieval Tradition in Christian, Muslim, and Jewish Art*, Religion and Arts 3 (Missoula, Mont., 1976).

22. Cf. Gutmann, "Kingdom Comes," pp. 173–75 and Joseph Gutmann "The Messiah at the Seder: A Fifteenth-Century Motif in Jewish Art," *Raphael Mahler Jubilee Volume*, ed. Samuel Yeivin (Tel Aviv, 1974), pp. 29–38.

1. The finding of Moses. Dura-Europos synagogue, west wall, ca. 245.

2. The finding of Moses. Haggadah, Catalonia, ca. 1320, British Library, Add. 27210, fol. 9.

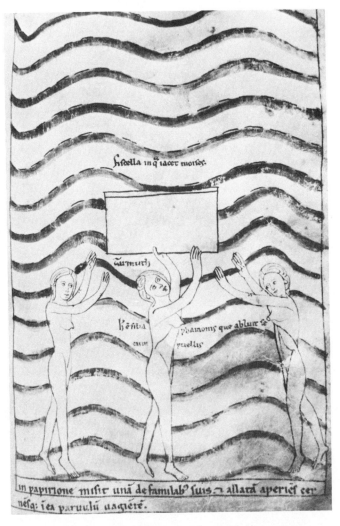

fiscella in q̄ iacet moisef.

aũ muidi

b̃ēba cum puellis

phamonis que ablu t̄

in papirione misir unā de familab' suis 7 allatā aperies cer
nesq: iea paruulū uagieré.

3. The finding of Moses. Bible, Pamplona, Spain, ca. 1200.
Harburg, Collection Prince Oettingen-Wallerstein, Ms I,2 lat.
4, fol. 49.

4. The Dura-Europos synagogue, west wall, ca. 245.

5. Abraham breaking idols. Queen Mary's Psalter, 14th century, British Library, Ms. Royal 2B VII, fol. 8.

6. Abraham breaking idols. al-Bīrūnī, *Chronology of Ancient Nations*, Edinburgh Univ. Library, Arabic Ms. No. 161, fol. 102v.

7. Abraham breaking idols. Haggadah, Spain, 14th cent. British Library, Add. 14761, fol. 36v.

8. Abraham rescued from the fire. Speculum Humanae Salvationis. Kremsmünster, Codex Cremifanensis 243, fol. 37.

9. Abraham rescued from the fire. Rashīd al-Dīn, Jāmiᶜ al-Tāwārīkh, Edinburgh University Library, Arabic Ms. No. 20, fol. 3v.

11. The Sacrifice of Isaac. Commentary on Bible. Würzburg, Germany, 1233, Munich, Bayrische Staatsbibliothek, Cod. Hebr. 5, fol. 18v.

10. Abraham rescued from the fire. Haggadah, Catalonia, ca. 1320. British Library, Add. 27210, fol. 3.

12. The Sacrifice of Isaac. Chancel, side relief.
Wechselburg, Marienkirche, early 13th century.

13. The Sacrifice of Isaac. Dura-Europos synagogue, ca.
245.

14. Messianic banquet. Bible. S. Germany, 13th century. Milan, Biblioteca Ambrosiana, Cod. B. 32 Inf. fol. 136.

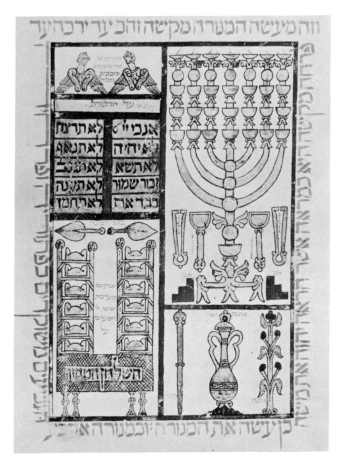

15-16. Messianic Temple. Bible. Perpignan, 1299. Paris, Bibliothèque Nationale, Ms. hébr. 7, fols. 12v-13.

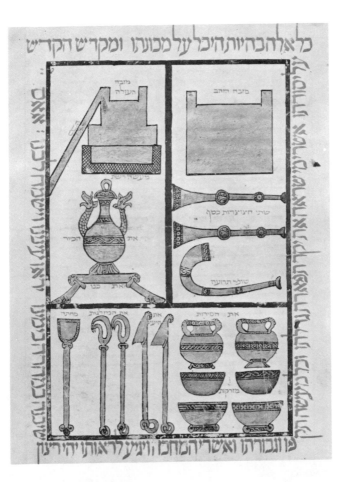

17. Water drawing device. al-Jazari, Treatise on Automata 13th century. Washington, D. C., Freer Gallery of Art, acc. no. 30.75.

18. Messiah at the Seder. Haggadah, North Italy, 1478. Washington, D. C., Library of Congress, fol. 19v.

19. Palmesel, S. Germany, late 15th century. Detroit Institute of Arts, Acc. No. 57.97.

WHY IS THE GRAIL

KNIGHT JEWISH?

A PASSOVER MEDITATION

Leslie A. Fiedler

Of all the legends, the communal dreams which have possessed the imagination of the West, that of the Grail seems the most tantalizing and evasive. It not merely remains—after eight hundred years of writing, rewriting, emendation, and commentary—contradictory, inchoate, and incomplete; but it slips maddeningly through the fingers of all who strive to possess it. It belongs finally to no one and to everyone: the critic and scholar, the prophet, the priest and the politician as well as the poet, the sculptor, and the illustrator of children's books. Most of all, however, it belongs to the children who read such books or listen to them being read aloud —or merely look at the pictures—and have blessedly never heard of Chrétien de Troyes or Wolfram or the Pseudo-Wachier or Malory.[1]

It is therefore in the voice of what survives in me of the child that I prefer to speak of the Grail: a child moved by wonder in the presence of a dream presumably first dreamed by others, but so like dreams he has already dreamed himself that he sometimes believed he had invented it; though, in fact, its wonder contained, as he somehow sensed from the start, a hint of terror, a threat.

At any rate, I feel committed to an attempt to re-dream that Passover dream as if it were my own; or to put it somewhat less metaphorically, to try to relocate the myth which exists before, after, outside all of the Christian texts which pretend to embody it, by demonstrating the sense in which it is a Jewish myth. Or perhaps I mean rather a myth about Jews: a reflection of the plight of my own people at a particular historical moment—recorded first by one who may have been a Jew converted to Christianity, and then revised by a score of gentiles, some more, some less aware of what in mythological terms they were doing. Think of Wolfram, for instance, who traced the ultimate origins of the myth to something the Jew Phlegetanis had read in the stars.

But how to locate the myth of the Grail is the question, since like all myths, it exists outside of any particular combination of words—exists first of all as an ever-expanding and changing set of magical names: Gawain and Perceval, Galahad and Bors, Joseph and Pelles and Bron. But also it preexists as a set of archetypal misadventures: the unasked question of the *schlemiehl* son, the mysterious wound of the invisible father, the failed first quest, and the inconclusive second chance. Ultimately, however, and primordially as well, the legend consists of a cluster of wordless images and ikons, called by names no one quite understands, like "Grail" itself.

At first even the number of the aboriginal ikons was unsure; though they focused finally to four clearly defined symbols—Cup and Lance, Sword and Dish—which in turn became pips on playing cards—diamonds and clubs, hearts and spades—as the dream which became literature (though it aspired first perhaps to the status of scripture) ended as an amusement, a parlor game. "But what does it all mean?" we are driven to ask, having learned from the discomfiture of the *schlemiehl* Knight not to keep silent about such matters. Whom does the Grail serve?

For a long time we have teased ourselves with the notion that if only we could see it all—the total pattern, the whole *gestalt*, the completed tale with a proper beginning and end—we would know. But we possess only fragments, scraps, "a heap of testimony," which is in Hebrew *Galaad*, the final name of the many-named Grail Knight. And at the beginning of it all there is the mysterious and contradictory poem of Chrétien de Troyes, the text of which hastens to assure us that it is not a beginning, that before it there was already a tradition written down in books, and which breaks off rather than concludes, presumably at the death of its author.

No wonder that the readers of Chrétien's fragmentary poem have most often felt it more challenging than satisfactory, an invitation to finish the tale and thus answer the questions it posed and left unanswered; or perhaps it would be better to say, using its own central metaphor, to find questions for the answers it left dangling. At any rate, almost immediately four or five poets, known and unknown, tried to finish the tale in Chrétien's own tongue; and before half a century had passed, there existed in prose and verse, in French and English and German, a half dozen major attempts to fill in the blanks, fore and aft, of a recorded dream, which perhaps by its very essence, had to, has still to blur away at the edges rather than be sharply focused.

Yet how hard it has proved for poets and scholars alike to accept the fact that being in the deepest sense popular fiction, the Grail story has *necessarily* neither a proper Aristotelian beginning nor end, but only an indefinitely extensible middle, like a soap opera or a comic strip. Moreover the attempt to end the essentially endless tale often, perhaps inevitably, implies a covert desire to capture it, use it, exploit it by euhemerizing or allegorizing its magic inconsequence in the interests of one cause or another: to promote the reform of monastic life, or to advertise a shrine, authenticate a relic, or support the bishops of Glastonbury against those of Canterbury, perhaps even to subvert the Roman Church by providing an alternative version of the apostolic succession and a new reading of Christ's symbolic transformation of the Passover Seder.

Such acts of appropriation did not end with the Middle Ages. Nineteenth-century artists as different from each other as Wagner, Tennyson, and William Morris have reworked the legend on behalf of German Naturalism, the sanctity of the bourgeois family, and artsy-craftsy socialism. Moreover in our own century John Cowper Powys has sought to bend the myth to serve his own eccentric neo-Welsh mysticism, while Charles Williams has redeployed it in the interests of antisemitism, the polite occult, and a genteel Anglicanism.

There has been one radical change in recent times, however, as, from the mid-nineteenth century, scholars began to contend with poets, artists, and priests for the right to complete, interpret, or appropriate the Myth. Typically, however, such scholars have (as is the habit of their trade) attempted to complete it by looking *backwards*, i.e., by finding the roots, the beginnings, something before Chrétien's eruption into print: if not that perhaps nonexistent book from the library of Philip of Flanders, to which he himself alludes, then a Celtic original, Welsh or Irish; at the very least some trace of a folk tale, some evidence of a prior religious rite or lapsed cult—*something*.

Diligent source-hunters have discovered presumable roots for the Grail legend in accounts of voyages to fairy land, in Greek mystery religions, the Jewish Kabbala, the Byzantine rite, the ceremonies of the martyred Cathares, the rituals of Free Masonry or of the Knights Templar, the cults of Attis and Adonis, and the worship of a burning glass as a symbol of the Holy Trinity. Sometimes the proponents of such theories have claimed to find survivals of such ancient cult practices in still living faiths ranging from Methodism to Rosicrucianism. Indeed for the most literal-minded devotees of the myth, the physical Grail still exists (though this relic of a faith institutionalized only in literature has been variously portrayed as a Stone, a Platter, and a Chalice) in regions as remote from each other as the abbey at Glastonbury and the castle of Mont Ségur, to which I made pilgrimages before I realized that I, too, was engaged in the vainest and most satisfactory of quests. In that quest strange allies have gathered together, including—if the *Morning of the Magicians* can be believed —Adolf Hitler, who planned an expedition to recover it from a remote hiding-place in Central Asia, revealed to him by one of his gurus, once the great war was won. But evoking the name of Hitler not only reminds us that the connection between antisemitism and the Grail has persisted from the start into our own time, but alerts us also to the fact that all seekers for the Grail tend to continue the story, imagining for it new endings as well as new beginnings.

Even the scholars, despite their primary interest in etiology, have become unworthy continuers of the legend, collaborators in the endless web of narrative the western world never ceases to spin around its central ikons. I refer not only to the sense in which all criticism implies a revision of the texts it pretends to explicate, or even to the way in which this is particularly true in the case of popular literature, to which in some deep sense the Grail story belongs; but chiefly to the specific case of Jessie Weston's *From Ritual to Romance*, the crowning work of a lifetime of Arthurian scholarship, which became an occasion for T.S. Eliot's *The Waste Land*, that key book of the modernist canon, which also evokes, *via* a tag from Verlaine, Wagner's reworking of the legend according to Wolfram von Eschenbach. Nor was that the end of the process; for if Eliot's poem connects back on the one hand to Miss Weston's scholarly study, which it thus makes retrospectively also a work of literature, a continuation of Chrétien, on the other hand it connects forward to Bernard Malamud's allegorical fiction, *The Natural*. Is it merely paradoxical, then, that the most ambitious poem of an ex-American antisemite should have been the source for the only (apparently) non-Jewish novel of a Jewish-American author, who has ever since made Jewishness his central theme? Or did Malamud perceive somehow, on some level of awareness, the centrality of Jewishness to the original Grail story, which Eliot did not, and, indeed, could not, pledged as he was to ban the "perfidious Jews" ("free-thinking Jews," he preferred to say) from his ideal commonwealth?

It is not, however, with the whole life-span of the twice-born Grail legend that I am centrally concerned, though its death in the High Renaissance and its rebirth during the later stages of romanticism is a subject I find fascinating and instructive. It is rather with the first fifty years of its first life, its infancy, or more properly, its early maturity, since it was born full-grown with Chré-

tien's *Perceval*. This means that I shall be dealing with
the Grail legend primarily as a product of the "Twelfth
Century Renaissance": a cultural phenomenon quite as
characteristic of that postmillennial time as the inven-
tion of the university, the final fruition of scholasticism,
the beginnings of modern urbanism, and the backlash
of the failed Crusades, which had set out to reclaim the
Holy Land and has ended by bringing back to Europe
leprosy and antisemitism. The twelfth century marks, I
am suggesting, the beginning of the end of tolerance or
quasi-tolerance of the Jews, even in such communities
as Troyes, where earlier they had moved freely, disputed
openly, owned property, and functioned almost, *almost*
as accepted members of the total community.

But the twelfth century was also the moment in which
the institution we have come to call "literature" was
first fully established. Vernacular poetry and prose dealing chiefly, or even exclusively, with secular concerns
like war and love and imbued with values non- or even
anti-Christian were barely a century old, when Chrétien
wrote the narrative in which the images and themes of
the Grail story surfaced for the first time. His language,
his music, his tone were derived from those of the secular romances with which indeed he had experimented
earlier; but his subject matter this time is, however am-
biguously, religious though not quite orthodox. I am,
indeed, convinced that his otherwise inexplicably influential narrative is an attempt to represent, by way of the
Grail legend, a crisis not only in the troubled relationship of "literature" to "Scripture," but also of the Old
Testament to the New, which is to say, of the surviving
Jewish community in Europe to the Holy Roman Catholic Church.

For many years, I must confess, I was aware of only
one half of the conflict reflected in the Grail story, i.e.,

between the values imposed on the imperfectly Christianized pagans of Western Europe by a proselytizing Faith, and those implicit in the Matter of Britain: that mass of story material neither Hellenic nor Hebraic, which had been released from the collective unconsciousness of Europe by the free fantasy permitted in the vulgar literatures. What I have become aware of only recently are the implications of that newly intensified conflict for the Jews, who were cast in the role of archetypal enemy twice over: not just as the killers of Christ, though they are, indeed, presented as such from Chrétien on, but also as the founders of Christianity, toward which nominally Christian Europeans continued for a long time (perhaps even as late as Hitler) to feel a profound ambivalence. That ambivalence they dared express only obliquely, in the extra-Scriptural mythology about the transmission of the Christian faith to the westernmost reaches of Europe which stands at the very center of the Grail legend. I am referring, of course, to the oddly melancholy, the profoundly antitriumphal saga of Joseph of Arimathea and the long line of Jews who succeeded him as Keepers of the Grail, right down to that oddly Jewish non-Jewish son of a Jewish mother, Galahad. I was disturbed by the sadness of the Grail story even as it had descended to me in simplified and expurgated versions of Malory's *Morte d'Arthur*.

I did not understand that sadness, knowing only that though I loved the rest of the Arthurian story, I hated the Grail quest, and especially its anticlimax in the adventures of the disturbingly effete and maidenly Galahad, who had a vision but won the love of no lady. Like —I felt sure—all other readers, my sympathies were with the resolute but faithful "sinner," Lancelot; and I did not understand why everyone did not stand up and declare that all had gone well until the intrusion of the

Grail had turned upside down the values of a world which until then had seemed the world of my own dreams, indeed of the dreams of all boys, even an already scholarly and scared small Jew reading about the Round Table in Newark, New Jersey.

On my way toward a deeper understanding, I came first to see how the Grail story, though integrated into the Arthurian framework and in one sense inseparable from it, represented a set of values not merely alien but fatally hostile to the codes of chivalry and courtly love which motivated Camelot—as alien and hostile as Jewish theocratic morality was to the ceremonial hedonism of the Celts. The Grail itself, whether we understand it as the Cup of the Passover Benediction, the Platter which held the Paschal Sacrifice, or the Plate in which the Unleavened Bread was displayed, I came to see was a symbol for the role of Judaism in subverting the chivalric codes and a way of life dependent on them. Seen in this light the myth of the Grail figures forth the doom of a lovely imperfect civilization based on the poeticizing of carnal passion and bloodshed, and unable finally (though the myth itself represents a gallant attempt) to assimilate either Jewish law or the Jewish dream of a Messiah in its Nazarene form.

I was, I think, originally led astray by such interpretations of the Grail myth as Jessie Weston's, which in attempting to identify it with the myth of the dying and reborn god ended by falsifying it completely. We do not really experience or remember the Grail legend, in whatever text we encounter it, as a joyous tale, a high comedy ending with the healing of a king and the restoration of fertility to a waste land, though, to be sure, its story line contains such elements.

Typically, the wounded king recovers only in order to die, and the Grail Knight, the deliverer, more often

than not does not reign over the world his achieved
quest has redeemed, but retires, withdraws, disappears
—taking with him into concealment the Grail itself.
This retirement leaves the world, as it were, doubly
desolate, bereft of its chief talisman and its last hero.
What is left after this double bereavement, which constitutes a kind of failed Second Coming, is neither
nothingness nor a New Heaven and a New Earth—
only the same old world (as I who read the story first
in the *Morte d'Arthur* can never forget) without the
Round Table, from which Knights sallied forth to right
its wrongs, and the great adulterous love of Lancelot
and Guinevere, which lightened for a little while its
darkness. It seems a high price to pay for the redemption of a single saint in armor; perhaps on some level
the whole tale constitutes a criticism, more dreamed
than formulated, of what the transplantation of the
Judaeo-Christian mythology had actually meant for the
West: the salvation of a handful of individuals and the
loss of a great secular glory.

In the most pathetic version of the tale, the point is
especially clear. In order for the final Grail Knight,
Galahad, to be born, the hitherto perfect warrior, Lancelot, befuddled by drink and magic, must betray his true
beloved, for whom he initially betrayed his true king. It
is in the bed of a Jewish girl that that final betrayal is
accomplished, and in that same bed she gives birth to
the Jewish son (descent according to Orthodox law being matrilineal) who is destined to defeat his *goyish*
father.

How as a child I hated that moment of defeat—hated
the downfall of the greatest knight in the world, the
greatest lover at the hands of one who, though begotten
in passion, never learned to love as a man loves, and

was not of this world from the moment he entered it. What would I have made of it all, I wonder now, if anyone had suggested to me then that the encounter of Galahad and Lancelot represented in allegory or projection the troubled nightmare occasioned by the transmission into Britain, the Ultimate West, of a strange new morality and an even stranger messianic myth by way of the first Jew who ever landed on its shores.

All of this may seem remote from the tale as its first teller told it, remote from the ironic, only intermittently religious poem of Chrétien de Troyes. But it took only a half century or less for the Jewish lineage of the Grail Knight (whether called Perceval or Galahad) to be clearly spelled out. Though Chrétien himself does not do so, he comes close toward the very end of the last Perceval episode in his poem; at the same point, in fact, when a presumably unmotivated antisemitic aside gives us pause, suggesting, if we do not too quickly dismiss it, that the Jews, the Jewish "Problem," the dispute of Church and Synagogue, the mystery of Israel as first defined by St. Paul, is somehow in the back of the poet's mind, if not at the center of his concern.

At first, however, Chrétien does not seem to know where he is going, or perhaps is determined to mislead his auditors. Certainly his tone is initially mocking, reflecting a kind of courtly condescension (not unlike that in Perrault's much later rendition of similar folk material) toward Breton-Welsh, Irish material he is reworking, stuff of remotely bardic origin, perhaps, but more recently transmitted and transformed by unlettered peasants.

In any event he seems to have felt a need to treat his material in a style we have come only recently to call "camp," though the practice is an ancient one—a way of coming to terms with stories for which one is ashamed to admit his secret love, by pretending to burlesque them.

Especially in the Perceval sections of his narrative Chrétien employs this hypocritical device. The other half of his split hero, Gawain, is a courtly figure sharing fully the vices and virtues of the poet's original aristocratic audience, and he, therefore, does not really demand such treatment. But Perceval is from the start an outsider, not only because he is a Welshman, which is to say, a stranger from the woods, but because he is a *naif* without a name, a muddleheaded mama's boy unsocialized by contact with older, more experienced male models. No wonder he cannot tell an armed Knight from an angelic messenger, and is constantly getting into trouble by using yesterday's good advice today. It is a standard comic device in put-down tales told by the sophisticated at the expense of ethnic or class outsiders.

Yet Perceval is finally transformed from an inarticulate *schlemiehl*, a prefiguration of that son mentioned in the Passover Seder, who is "unable even to ask," to a kind of hero—if not quite a tragic hero, at least a disturbingly problematical figure. But his transformation occurs inadvertently, by mistake, as it were, when, without knowing what he is doing, he manages to kill his mother by the simple process of leaving home. It is like an old Jewish joke actualized into terror; the conventional threat of the Jewish mother ("Believe me, my son, if you go away from me, I'll drop dead!") becomes fact.

But the threat fulfilled means the transformation of Perceval's mother from a kind of Mrs. Portnoy *ante lettera* into the archetypal mother of us all, Rachel who weeps for her children and will not be comforted. By the same token it means the metamorphosis of a naive runaway boy into a kind of anti- or counter-Oedipus. Twice over Perceval is told (to the annoyance, I gather, of some scholars) that his inability to ask the proper question at the proper moment is due to his guilt for having, however unwittingly, slain his mother. But the two events, I am convinced, are tied together not accidentally but necessarily, which is to say, structurally, mythologically, archetypally; since the mystery of an answer-without-a-question is associated with mother murder even as the question-without-an-answer (the riddle of the Sphinx) is with father murder.

What I am suggesting has been suggested several times before, most notably by the eminent French anthropologist, Claude Lévi-Strauss in his inaugural address at the College de France. It seems apt that it be a Jewish prophet once more who has most convincingly argued that the Grail Legend is the complement, the binary opposite of the story of Oedipus, the Jewish antithesis to a Greek thesis. What is evoked is incest avoided rather than achieved; for as Lévi-Strauss goes on to explain of the Oedipus myth, "between the puzzle solution and incest there exists a relationship. Like the solved puzzle, incest brings together elements doomed to remain separate." The unsolved puzzle, on the other hand, betokens the maintaining of that separation. Ironically, however, it can only reverse the tragic oedipal dénouement, not resolve it comically.

The mother, fled from, dies and the father is resurrected, or at least restored to sexual potency—but only if the question is asked to complete the riddle whose answer preexists. It is a Judaeo-Christian paradox based on a Jewish joke. In light of all this, it is especially fitting that Chrétien's hero end up in the Grail Castle, an oddly displaced replica of the Temple of the Jews, as scholars have been pointing out ever since Moses Gaster.

Moreover within its walls, a transmogrified Passover Seder[2] is being enacted in orthodox Jewish style: the plate of the paschal sacrifice lifted aloft, the candles lit, the stage set in fact for the youngest male present, who is Perceval, to ask the traditional question, which of course he does not. So pure is he, so uninitiated, so sexually ignorant that he cannot even ask, like the Simple Son of the Paschal Haggadah, *"Mah zeh?"*, "What is it?" And so the springtime, whose coming is celebrated at the most literal level of the allegorical Passover ritual, never arrives. What is endured instead is what Lévi-Strauss calls "an eternal winter . . . pure to the point of sterility"—the baleful opposite of the Theban "eternal summer . . . licentious to the point of sterility."

The implication of Perceval's failure seems to me clear, though Chrétien apparently did not feel the necessity of spelling it out. If the virgin quester had asked at the failed Seder "Whom does the Grail serve?"; or if he were to be given a second chance and ask it at last, what he would have been or would be told is what is always told when the ritual question is asked, and "the periodicity of the seasonal rhythm" would be delivered from ascetic restraints without being permitted to lapse into orgiastic excess. It is the past on which the living feed in order to produce the yet unborn who will feed them by ritual remembrance. But this means in a Christian poem of the late Middle Ages that the seeker for a Second Coming will be told that the Grail serves the wounded old man in the further room, who though sterile now is the quester's own ancestor, which is to say, a Jewish Patriarch. The whole transaction symbolizes what is otherwise figured forth in the giving of manna: a sign that even in the desert, the waste land, God feeds his Chosen People. Not them alone, however, as the Passover Seder reminds us, opening as it does with the cry: "Let those who are hungry come in and eat." But them first of all—and the others, the gentiles, only through them, their election and their casting away, which extends but does not annul the promise sealed with the circumcision.

In Chrétien's poem Perceval learns that he is descended from the rich Fisher King through the mother he denied and killed; but it is not made explicit that this archetypal, undying male ancestor is himself Jewish. For that, the legend of Joseph of Arimathea, the Jewish Refugee who bore the relics of the Crucifixion to the West, had to be interwoven with the other strands of the tale. In the process the sacrificial platter assumed yet one more level of significance, being transformed into the Kiddush Cup of the Last Supper, without losing its other ceremonial meanings. But this has already been accomplished by the time of the first continuation of Chrétien's unfinished poem, at least in a passage considered by some to be an interpolation in the text. It is here that we first read how Joseph of Arimathea, after, like any good Jew, blowing a horn and ceremoniously washing his hands, sits down to the feast provided by Grail. When it is finished, we are told that he prays to God that neither glory nor the Grail pass from his line. "And," the author continues, "thus it befell. . . . For after Joseph's death no man had possession of it unless he was of Joseph's lineage. In truth the Rich Fisher descended from him, and all his heirs, and, they say, Guillem Guenelaus and his son Perceval."

From then on the tradition of the Jewishness of the Grail Knight was set; nor is it disturbed when Perceval is replaced at the center of the story by Galahad. As a matter of fact the mythological ante is raised by the switch, since in Galahad's case the Jewish roots of the Grail Knight are extended even further back along the

Messianic line of descent so that in the *Queste de San-grall*, Galahad is described on his first arrival at Arthur's Court, not merely as one "of King's lineage and of the kindred of Joseph of Arimathea," but also as "the desired Knight who is descended from high lineage of King David."

But why, one is drawn to ask, this palpable effort twelve hundred years after Christ to remythologize the Last Supper, to reinvent the *Meshiah ben David*, to re-imagine the mission of the Jews in the gentile world? The clue is, I think, to be found in a passage to which I have already alluded, and which has always troubled me especially because it is so essential a part of the nearest thing to a true conclusion to Chrétien's account of Perceval: an immediate prologue to his taking Easter Communion and his dismissal with the tantalizing phrase, "of him the tale tells no more." After a series of misadventures, beginning with the fiasco in the Grail Castle, that not-quite-hero had lapsed, according to this account, into a state of unawareness more abysmal than his first stupidity. So total is his amnesia, his unlearning of the difficult lessons he has so perilously learned, that he is found wandering abroad fully armed on Good Friday, accoutred for bloodshed like "the Jews and the sinners who slew" Christ on that day. Indeed, a Knight who encounters him by chance is so outraged at his gross behavior that he cries out in reproach: "Dear good sir, do you not believe in Jesus Christ, who wrote the New Law and gave it to the Christians. . . . The wicked Jews, whom one should kill like dogs, wrought their own harm and our good when they raised him to the cross. Themselves they destroyed, and us they saved." It is a blood-chilling phrase, spoken presumably on behalf of one who had preached the forgiveness of our enemies: "whom one should kill like dogs."

Actually Chrétien has earlier praised, in the prologue to his poem, the supreme Christian virtue of charity, and some latter-day scholars have even insisted that this is the central theme of the work. But there is little enough charity displayed in this gratuitous incitement to a pogrom, this encapsulated but virulent version of the "Mystery of Israel": the paradox that the salvation of the gentiles was achieved only at the price of the casting away of the Jews, which seems, on the face of it, a special occasion for that virtue.

Chrétien might well have read only shortly before, as Urban T. Holmes has reminded us, the seventy-ninth sermon of St. Bernard on the subject, of which there was a copy in the library of his patron Philip. Indeed the notion of Israel as the "mother" of Christianity may have come to him from that source, but he did not respond to its plea for understanding and tolerance. "The great charity of the Church," Bernard preached, "does not wish to withhold its delights from the rival Synagogue. . . . This is marvellous, that salvation is from the Jews. The Saviour has returned to the place whence he came for that the remnants of Israel may be saved. The branches are not ungrateful to the root, nor the sons to the mother . . . and thus all of Israel may be saved."

This is, of course, (except for the mother-son metaphor) standard Pauline doctrine as argued in the Epistle to the Hebrews 11, but Christian Europe needed to be reminded of it in the twelfth century; for even as Chrétien was writing, Jewish refugees were flocking into Troyes from outlying small towns, where rioting Christians were in fact threatening to "kill them like dogs." Among those refugees was the grandson of Rashi, eminent rabbi and commentator on the Scriptures, who two generations before had made Chrétien's native city a center of Jewish learning, in some sense a Jewish city.

There are some who argue that Chrétien had himself
been born a Jew; and indeed his name is one frequently
given to converts. But there is no conclusive evidence,
and finally that issue is of small importance, since in any
case he must have known Jews, exchanged greetings
with them, perhaps conversed and argued with them.
Certainly he could not have been ignorant of the growing terror that threatened them in his native place.

Indeed his poem reflects at its deepest levels, at precisely those places where personal anguish and religious
commitment break through his defensive irony and
courtly condescension, an awareness of that crisis. It is
not just an explosion of hatred which concludes the
Perceval episode of his poem, though it is that also, but
a confession as well of the guilt bred by the long in-
ternecine struggle of Christians and Jews over which
were the true Grail bearers, the authentic continuers of
the tradition and inheritors of the Promise. If, as Chrétien suggests, mythologically, archetypally speaking, all
Jews are guilty of deicide, all Christians, as Bernard
implies, are inadvertent matricides simply for having
abandoned the Synagogue; and they compound their
primal crime by murdering, or advocating the murder
of those who still remain faithful to the maternal cult.
Having thus killed Rachel, they are forever impotent,
capable perhaps of imagining the ultimate mystery, of
seeing in the mind's eye the Grail, borne typically in
the legend, I remind you, by a woman, who represents
typically, I suggest, what is feminine in the Divine, the
Great Mother, but not of touching it, possessing it—
being fed by it as the child is fed at the maternal breast.

In Chrétien's version of the story, there is no Galahad
—no second Saviour, who kills his gentile father to
avenge his Jewish mother, and, completing the ritual,
sees the Grail that has kept alive his maternal male an-

cestors. In any case that second Saviour saves nothing and feeds no one but himself, incapable of fertilizing the world with his icy virginity, so that finally he symbolizes a Second Coming even more inconclusive than the first. This later version of the Grail story is, however desperate, at least a Christian fable; Chrétien's earlier account takes from Christianity chiefly its anti-Jewishness, remaining an elegy for Celtic myth and courtly values with antisemitic overtones, the saddest, perhaps, of all comic poems. But it is fitting, after all, that a work which ended by denying charity it had begun by evoking, denying it specifically to God's Chosen People, and thus contributing in its own small way to the centuries of persecution which lay ahead for the Jews of Europe, should at its most memorable moments be a poem about failure: the tragicomic failure of the *goyim* to live by the code they had learned first from Israel, and with which, to speak the truth, they have not yet come to terms.

NOTES

1. The vast literature on Chrétien and on the Grail legend is rather formidable. A beginner might choose Urban T. Holmes, *Chrétien de Troyes* (New York, 1970) for his first book or perhaps, more ambitiously, Roger Sherman Loomis et al., *Arthurian Literature in the Middle Ages* (Oxford, 1959). Other important works are Jean Frappier, *Le Roman Breton: Chrétien de Troyes, Perceval ou le Conte du Graal* (Paris, 1953); Henry R. and Renee Kahane, *The Krater and the Grail, Hermetic Studies of the Parzifal* (Urbana, 1965); M. Amelia Klenke, *Liturgy and Allegory in Chrétien's Perceval*

(Chapel Hill, 1951); Leonardo Olschki, *The Grail Castle and its Mysteries* with a Preface by Eugene Vinaver, tr. J.A. Scott (Manchester, 1966); Jessie L. Weston, *From Ritual to Romance* (Cambridge, 1920); Jean Frappier, *Chrétien de Troyes, l'Homme et l'Oeuvre* (Paris, 1957); Urban T. Holmes and Amelia Klenke, *Chrétien, Troyes and the Grail* (Chapel Hill, 1959). William Roach has edited *Le Roman de Perceval* (Paris, 1959); an easily accessible translation of *Perceval* is in Roger Sherman and Laura Hibbard Loomis, ed., *Medieval Romances* (New York, 1957).

2. Since writing this paper, I have read a dissertation, done at Cornell University by Eugene J. Weinraub, which works out in much greater detail the correspondence between the Grail Procession and the Passover Seder. See Eugene J. Weinraub, *Chrétien's Jewish Grail: A New Investigation of the Imagery and Significance of Chrétien de Troyes' Grail Episode Based upon Medieval Hebraic Sources*, University of North Carolina Studies in the Romance Languages and Literatures: Essays, No. 2 (Chapel Hill, 1976).

DISPUTATIO

Sunday, 5 May 1974

PARTICIPANTS

Chairman, Edward A. Synan, Pontifical Institute of
    Mediaeval Studies
Jeremy duQ. Adams, Southern Methodist University
Norman Cantor, New York University
Alice M. Colby-Hall, Cornell University
Stanley Ferber, State University of New York at Bing-
    hamton

PAUL E. SZARMACH, CONFERENCE COORDINATOR:

This morning's session is a *disputatio*, which is tech-
nically a medieval philosophical debate. We are mod-
erns, and we will make some adjustments in that rather
traditional method of dispute and discourse. We do not
have a round table; I must therefore use alphabetical
order as a means of precedence with one exception, our
disputatio moderator and leader Father Synan.

I would like to turn the proceedings to Father Synan
who will explain our method of procedure this morning
and who will conduct the proceedings from this point.
Father Synan.

FATHER SYNAN:

As Professor Szarmach indicated, we are doing our best
to set up this morning a twentieth-century analogue to
the *Questio Disputata de Quolibet* of the thirteenth
century. Because we are doing it in terms of analogy
rather than of univocity, we are making several changes
in the way those old boys did their business. The first
change is that this morning I should like very, very
briefly to express the appreciation of those of us who
are guests at SUNY for these days for their combination of courtesy and competence in a very special way:
Paul Szarmach, François Bucher, and Professor Bernard
F. Huppé, who is with us this morning after what seems
to have been a transitory indisposition. With this pro-
fessorial phalanx out of the way, I should also like to
thank Mr. Lansdown, the man who is taking care of
transportation this morning. He is very tall, very con-
spicious; tall people always impress me for some obscure, possibly Freudian reason, but I have observed his
activity with admiration now for two days.

Now the medieval disputation, which we are trying to
imitate or to mine for whatever value it may have, derives no doubt from very complex sources from which I
think we cannot exclude the possibility that rabbinic
disputations played their role. In any case Aristotle certainly was there; Aristotle was the one who told me how
to pose the question. The question must always be an-
swerable in terms of either yes or no. If you can't formulate your question that way, you are not allowed to ask
it. So this is what Aristotle had in mind. We are going
to ignore that prescription this morning. Furthermore
the disputation was the work of the master; and the
master, you will be perhaps a little terrified to know,
had as his first and most noble function, not to carry on

disputations at all but to preach. *Praedicare* was where the master began, but marked as I am by my very clothing this morning as a persecuted minority figure, I am going to dispense with that role of the master. The next thing he was supposed to do was, he was supposed to go in for something called *legere*—he was supposed to "read." Now this rather odd verb, because it really meant that he was supposed to talk, is maintained in the British University system. You have the reader in crystalography for the university and you do even on this continent give "lectures," and these are visible traces of the role of *legere*; but the liveliest thing he did was *disputare*, and the disputation of the medieval university took place in two ways. First of all you had *disputatio ordinaria*, and this was an organized teaching device that went on all year long, semester by semester, but in addition to that you had a more difficult one, because it was so difficult it was actually voluntary, and this was the *disputatio de quolibet*—a disputation in which you were allowed to put your name on the board and announce "I shall dispute on anything." And then the considerable ingenuity of staff and students was exercised against you, and they would ask you various silly questions to which you were obliged to give formal answers. This morning I think we are more or less in the role of the *disputatio de quolibet*. This morning it isn't part of an ordered, organic, systematic intellectual formation. We are simply here and we are going to say pretty well anything we like. However we will have to structure it. So, since medieval university disputations always had a lot of pros and cons, we have four professional naysayers who have been introduced to you in alphabetical order seated at the table. The first thing we are going to ask them to do this morning is to undertake, for about ten minutes apiece, to say anything they like about any paper they have heard. Now this really is *disputatio de quolibet* with a vengeance.

Since the medieval university did allow the nay-sayer to say his "nays," they also allowed for the man who said "yes" and consequently, when that is over, we are going to spend about equal time with those who delivered their papers. The men who delivered their papers, I have been urged to inform, may do so, if they like, from the aisles where there are microphones or they may, if they wish, come down here and speak from the lectern. We will ask them to keep their remarks to about ten minutes. Now this may be a heroic renunciation on the part of one or another, but we are going to admire them.

JEREMY DUQ. ADAMS:

Thank you. I think one of the pleasures as well as one of the problems of this whole conference has been the extraordinary variety of discourse—of styles and genres as well as individual addresses—which we have been facing and reacting to and thinking about since Friday evening. This morning I would like to respond in particular to two of the speakers, Rosemary Ruether and Harriet Goldberg, although I think (if this is not too sexist a reaction) that I was most particularly struck by the speeches of Yosef Yerushalmi and Leslie Fiedler. Concerning Leslie Fiedler's, I would like to reveal that as I lay in the Holiday Inn last night (an appropriate place to be on Friday and Saturday nights and Sunday mornings), I was vouchsafed a dream—a revelation in which I was enabled to see how Mr. Fiedler's analysis of the Grail Knight's problem allows us to understand finally, in a systematic and structured way, not simply the Grail legend but in a larger sense all the speeches of this conference, which I think can be seen as a myth in its own right, writing itself out in all of us. If anyone would like to share my revelation, say in the third round, I would be delighted to convey it. But there is more serious business at hand in the way of specific and substantive observations.

The thing that struck me most forcefully and most disturbed me in Professor Yerushalmi's speech is that it seemed, as I listened to it unfold, to preempt most of the critical business that, having read some of the papers in advance, I thought I should be addressing myself to. As he listed some of the things we don't need more of, speech after speech of the rest of this conference appeared either to fall by the wayside or suddenly to become a target for a dart. Does not his sense of the most valuable direction of Judaica preclude several of the kinds of studies with which we have been presented here—and which I must confess I have found instructive? What about, first of all, the question of Jewish contribution to gentile culture? A speculation about the Grail Knight's fundamental problem is clearly just such a paper. Am I going beyond Yerushalmi's own language when I see Ms. Ruether's speech as an instance of the further breast-beating of the repentant Christian? I think that was an important statement to make, but it has intellectual problems on its own, besides fitting one of Yerushalmi's categories. Although I very much enjoyed Professor Stillman's speech about the Golden Age of Spanish Jewry under Islamic rule, I wonder if it is not another example of the kind of parallel-tracking to which Professor Yerushalmi expressed his objections. In any case I was personally grateful for the parallel-tracking information that Spanish Jews as well as Spanish Muslims and Spanish Christians were given to a kind of hyperorthodoxy, not only in religion but also in culture, especially literary culture, and also to a rather special kind of genealogical consciousness. That's the kind of thing that my own instincts drive me to look for, and I must wonder if that instinct sets both Professor Stillman and me irretrievably at variance with Yosef Yerushalmi's otherwise very moving appeal; I hope not.

To that appeal I have only one substantive objection. In one sentence Yosef Yerushalmi referred briefly, as indeed the whole conference has tended, to something called "the patristic position"—a highly traditional label, indeed, canonical. Since I deal in that field, I suppose it is not surprising that I don't find it an adequate label. I recognize that lots of venerable labels can be seen as inadequate by those who work nitpickingly within their purview—"feudalism," for example, or "romanticism"—but I do think it's fair to protest that the term "patristic" has got to cover an excessively huge and diverse zone of historical and intellectual phenomena. "Patristic" must do service first of all for two great linguistic traditions, the Latin and the Greek—indeed for a third, the Syriac. It is made to apply over several centuries to a great variety of regions and cultural states, to an enormous variety of personal styles, and so on. I don't actually take strong exception to that one phrase in Yerushalmi's speech, although when he insisted that we have to ask the questions "which Jew?" in "which city?" in "which kind of role?" in "which kind of country?", I was tempted to remark that we really ought to ask "which Father?" whenever we are about to describe something as "patristic" or "nonpatristic."

That, I suppose, is my basic general objection to the contribution of this conference, and that objection to the conception of the patristic registered most severely in connection with the papers of Rosemary Ruether and

Harriet Goldberg. I don't really want to say too much
about Ms. Ruether's speech, partly because I feel so very
uncomfortable with it. I neither want to fall into something resembling a Christian apology for a position to
which I am not in fact sympathetic, nor do I want to get
involved in some kind of masculine/feminine conflict.
I hope it is appropriate, however, to say at least that I
was disturbed, and that I wish Rosemary Ruether were
here so that one could be more candidly in opposition.

What disturbed me was her treatment of several
topics, which frankly struck me as approaches to carica-
ture, more destructive than useful in a number of ways.
The category "patristic" seemed to me more abused than
usual in that speech; the most acute case of that abuse
was John Chrysostom. That patriarch is not one of the
favorites of progressive-minded Christians of the present day and was certainly not one of the favorite Christians of the Jewish tradition. Harriet Goldberg has
revealed in a delicious footnote (no. 19, which I regret
the audience was not able to enjoy) how Chrysostom
was presented by a later (I suppose Jewish) tradition in
Spain as a man who practiced what he preached against
in some very interesting and indecent ways. Chrysostom
is a problematic figure. He was a rhetorician who indulged in the kind of diatribe common to his generation
—indeed standard for several centuries in either direction—and did it with verve and finesse; it is a talent that
makes him difficult for us to enjoy. I have no desire to
try exculpating Chrysostom for his very clear anti-Jewish
sentiments, but I do think it less than useful to the historical enterprise, to the intellectual enterprise in general, to present him as just another voice in a network of
loudspeakers enunciating the same repellent anti-Jewish
theme, rather than to try to see which specific situations
prompted this specific outburst of that deplorable mes-

sage. I think this is particularly important because Chrysostom is one of the Fathers who responded most vivid-
ly to a given impulse. A fine example is his set of
sermons on the so-called Incident of the Statues, which
in that tendency to dominant concreteness are very much
like his set of sermons against the presence of Jewish
proselytism as he met it in Constantinople. Our theme
here would be better served by exploring that concrete,
authentically Jewish event (whether factual or alleged),
by savoring the particular coloration of this outburst of
Chrysostom's, than by graying him out into some "patristic" profile.

The second problem with Rosemary Ruether's speech
is an extension of the first: a tendency to rigid categorical overstatement. I find this especially curious in a
scholar who speaks so movingly against categorical
errors on the part of modern Christian commentators as
well as of patristic exegetes. Perhaps it might be useful
later to talk a little bit more about her use of words like
"cultural obliteration." "Cultural obliteration is programmed into Christianity:" that may indeed be true; I
am not sure I find it very useful at the moment. It seems
to me almost as little useful to the concerns of this conference as Ms. Ruether's attack on John Foster Dulles's
kind of Christian Messianic foreign policy (although
that *was* an aside, and not part of the original manuscript). What really bothers me is that she presents
genocide as programmed right into the core of a Christian "dualism." Genocide is usually a policy chosen by
monistic societies which want to wipe out those who
disagree. In general dualistic societies distinctly prefer
to keep around the scapegoat crucial to their own self-
definition. The treatment of deviants in Puritan New
England is just one instance of this tendency: occasional
burnings, but no genuine, sustained attempt to remove.

With Harriet Goldberg's speech I find myself in strong sympathy. I like it very much and want for that reason alone to offer one observation on the "patristic" line: I hope we can fight about it usefully before all this goes to press. I refer to her query: "Is it necessary to establish to any reader of patristic literature that the Church had two enemies beside Satan—Jews and women?" A burst of appreciative laughter greeted this opening presentation of a great issue. I shared the audience's appreciation of Ms. Goldberg's rhetoric, but I am afraid that this is one reader of patristic literature for whom that does need to be established.

I am sure that you can find writers who are authentically "patristic" and talk as though the Church had three prime enemies: Satan, the Jews, and women. They would probably be the very writers best remembered by a literary tradition which enjoys humor and dirty stories and either ironic or negative thematic material. But I would have thought that if we went searching through the body of patristic literature—western patristic literature, that is—to find a classic treatment of the Church and her enemies, we would have to focus on *The City of God*. If we look there, I simply cannot find that kind of structure anywhere in the book. It has antisemitic remarks, it has a variety of unpleasant things of that sort, but it seems to me that the fundamental structure of *The City of God's* statement on that question goes something like this: the enemy of the *civitas Dei* (which is the transcendent form of the Church) is the *civitas terrena*, the Earthly City; sometimes, though not too frequently, Augustine does call that the *civitas diaboli*. But what does he mean by that attribution? Does he mean that the Devil inspires that City, shapes it, or has formed it? I think he means rather that the Devil provides occasional propaganda and leads it onward; he is just waiting for it to come into his own domain in the end. The real enemy of the Church, it appears to me (not just to me: it's pretty much the common scholarly critique) is fundamentally not a type, like the Jew, the woman, or the Devil, but a force—*libido*, an extraordinarily common and universal force. Specifically it's the *libido dominandi*, the lust to rule, the lust to dominate. As Augustine presents and concretizes this particular "fundamental enemy" of mankind, not simply of the Church, he tends to illustrate it not by Jews and women, but by emperors and generals who are distinctly male and gentile. It seems to me that those illustrations are a more important statement about the real threat to the Church than the half-hearted, lackluster praises of Theodosius and various Roman emperors in the recent past (in the end of book V).

One final point in connection with this. I like very much the idea that the sense of the woman and the sense of the Jew threatened the male clerical image-makers of post-*Reconquista* Spain. I have found very much the same kind of thing in my current research on pre-Arabic Spain in the ideology of the Visigothic elite. I welcome very much the kind of insights from the other side of those two great Conquests that Harriet Goldberg has offered us; I only wish that her research would lead her, perhaps even in this paper, to look a little bit deeper for the LCD, the Lowest Common Denominator. I don't think it's wiliness or *superbia* or any of those key sins which all tend to mush into one another anyway in Gregory the Great's psychological machinery. I have the feeling that it's something much deeper, which would enhance her thesis rather than hurting it: that is, pollution. If we could push that suggestion a bit further and even get Lévi-Straussian, I think that might be fun. Thank you.

NORMAN F. CANTOR:

I see I am down to two duties this morning: first of all
to participate in the initial phase of the disputation, and
then to try to sum up the whole performance, the whole
discussion this morning. In case people think I have completely lost my senses, how I got involved in the latter,
trying to sum up the whole morning, is that at 11:25
last night, waking me from a very deep sleep, Mr.
Bucher phoned me to invite me to do this. When I got
up this morning, I was sure this was a part of a very
fantastic nightmare. When I got here, I discovered it
was all too true.

I take the term "disputation" literally. While noting
the many excellent things we have heard in the last two
days and giving due credit to ideas and perceptions I
found particularly valuable, I want to stress points I dis-
agreed with or at least questioned or think need elaboration. If I seem at times ungenerous or even aggressive
or mean, it is not for lack of appreciation for the learning and insight of our panel of speakers, I assure you.

Mr. Yerushalmi's paper seemed to stop just about
where I had hoped it would begin. I expected an assessment of the recent and current work in Jewish history
and a historiographical analysis of the work of scholars
like Baer, Baron, Gerson Cohen, Gershom Scholem,
Goitein, and Ellis Rifkin. I expected a study of what
had been done on Jewish history, the variety of interpretation, the variety of insights into medieval Jewish culture and society. Now here are some remarks inspired
by what Mr. Yerushalmi did say. "Perhaps," as he says,
"there has been too exclusive use of archival records, and
this too exclusive use makes medieval Jews to be all
court Jews." But I would say that the court Jews were
crucially important, not only in politics and taxation,

but also in culture and thought, as Mr. Stillman's paper brought out.

As far as I can see, medieval Jewry was in effect a one-class society. There was one courtly, rabbinical, literary, mercantile elite, and all Jews besides this immensely wealthy, prominent, fortunate, learned elite were the silent exploited masses. Exploited and repressed I think, not only by the Gentiles, but also by the dominant court Jews. Everytime I read or hear about medieval Jewry, I think of Hannah Arendt's *Eichmann in Jerusalem* and her unforgettable picture of how the Jewish masses of Hungary were sold into the Nazi gas chambers by the Budapest Jewish community leaders, so many of whom survived to become American businessmen or indeed Israeli officials. If we are going to talk of the inner development of medieval Jewry, can we please talk about the class structure, the deprivation of the Jewish masses, the control of community institutions by the courtly, rabbinical, mercantile elite: the way in which the rich, well-born and learned Jews often survived even pogroms and moved easily on to havens in other countries while the masses in bad times sank even further into poverty, misery, and martyrdom? When will Jewish historians start to tell us frankly that the misery of Jews is not only the guilt of Gentiles? When will we be asked to contemplate the eternal peril of Jews without money, without learning, without easy mobility? We have already indeed been asked to do so in a bold but too schematically Marxist book by Ellis Rifkin and in a truly great book by Rafael Mahler of Tel Aviv University, the best book I have ever read on the social history of the Jewish Diaspora, which is a monumental study of the European Jewish communities at the end of the eighteenth century.

Mr. Yerushalmi condemns parallels, but at the same

time, he wants a truly universal history with Jews and
Judaism in proper role and perspective. I can't see how
he can have it both ways. Of course there are overly
facile parallels that aren't very useful, but even the case
he mentions, of making Maimonides the Jewish Aquinas, isn't very useless and isn't false. Maimonides was
the Jewish Aquinas and Aquinas himself knew that. But
sophisticated parallels, or what I would call interpreting
Jewish history in terms of behavioral models common
to all historical understanding, using the general categories of historical and sociological explanation, are
absolutely necessary to make any sense out of the Jewish past. And examples of such general models are not
only class configuration and struggle and social mobility,
which I have already referred to, but such models as
the following: spiritual and apocalyptic revivalism,
puritanism, socialization and acculturation, functional
utility of institutions, *anomie*, romanticism, cultural
crisis, leadership patterns, alienation. With respect to
alienation Mr. Yerushalmi is persuasive in his criticism
of the simple typology of Jew as wanderer and stranger,
but this is by no means the only kind of alienation that
exists in Jewish or any other kind of history. Alienation
is a psychosocial condition that separates the individual
from his society and his communal history, his communal past. It represents the deracinization of the individual, the taking away from his roots, and reflects the
severe dysfunctioning of familial and group institutions.
This alienation is the most obvious fact of American
Jewish history. I would guess it was not rare in the
Middle Ages. It is not clear from Mr. Yerushalmi's talk
exactly what he considers the use of Jewish history to
be for Jews, why he wants to discover the inner development of the medieval Jewish world. At times I sensed a
tone entering his talk of that militant cultural and ethnic

nationalism that has recently inspired and, in my view, all but wrecked Afro-American history. But perhaps I misunderstand him and do him an injustice.

In any case the use of Jewish history for Jews at the present time is suggested by Mr. Stillman's learned and subtle essay. The use of the intense study of the medieval Jewish past is, I believe, to identify, to rediscover and revivify alternative Jewish traditions, those traditions that are alternative to rabbinical and nationalistic Judaism. The triumph eventually repressed the other modes of Jewish behavior and experience and today are foisted upon us as *per se echt* "Judaism." What I am saying is that Mr. Stillman's study of medieval Andalusian Jewry reveals, as such other studies reveal, that to think of rabbinism and Zionism as the only valid Jewish historical traditions is wrong, although the rabbis and the Zionists want us to believe this gross falsification of the Jewish past. From Mr. Stillman's paper we can certainly see the importance, perhaps indeed the coming triumph of Talmudic Judaism with its exclusivist, puritan, and rabbi-dominated attitude; and we can see perhaps in ha-Levi the coming of nationalism, an almost inevitable response to Muslim, and Christian militancy. But we can also perceive alternative Jewish heritages, which are inspiring, fascinating, equally valid models of Jewish experience, and these are: first, courtly aristocratic culture involving romantic individualism. "This is the sign of the covenant between us," Mr. Stillman's poet celebrates as he holds up the cup of wine. And this aristocratic culture involves the intense exploration of all forms of liberating sexuality, heterosexuality, bisexuality, homosexuality. Ask your average suburban rabbi his views on homosexuality and he will tell you there is nothing more un-Jewish than this, oy-veh. But not if you study Spanish Jewish culture. Homosexuality is central

to it. At the present time we have more than a surfeit
of middle class Jewish liberal culture. We have a nau-
seating surplus of Jewish leftism. Time at least to restore the balance and recover some of the grand, aristocratic, courtly, romantic, highly sexual Jewish tradition.
Second, sufism-mysticism, à la Ibn Pakuda, leading on,
I assume, as it picks up magical and astrological strands,
to sixteenth-century Kabbalism, which Gershen Scholem
has shown to be the richest and most vibrant Jewish
culture of the premodern Diaspora. And this culture,
much narrowed and impoverished, was still perpetuated
in modern Hassidism. Third, eschatological, messianic,
and apocalyptic movements, not political apocalypti-
cism, which leads eventually to the confusion and misery that you have in Israel today, but spiritual apocalyp-
ticism. Fourth, Karaism, that wonderful, puritanical, (I
have always suspected) *petit bourgeois* and perhaps
working-class faith that was so brutally repressed by the
rabbinate because it threatened the authority of the
courtly rabbinical merchant elite. Karaism, about which
so little is yet known and which has totally passed out
of the collective Jewish memory. How richer, how more
dramatic, how more appealing to intellectuals, to artists,
to students, to the young, to women, would Jewish life
be today if these four traditions I have listed were
strong and influential in addition to rabbinism and
Zionism. It is the first duty of the historian of the Jewish Middle Ages, I think, to concentrate upon these
alternative heritages and to put them before the Jewish
public as fully authentic forms of Jewish experience and
behavior. . . . Of course in so doing they will anger the
rabbis and the Zionists, but they yet may save Jewish
life from decay and disintegration, and they may save it
from the moral and spiritual suffocation that is currently so evident; and they may provide the intellectual

foundations for the Jewish Renaissance and Reformation. Remember that all good history is subversive and undermines the establishment.

ALICE COLBY-HALL:

I will address my comments to Professor Fiedler's paper, since I too have a long-standing interest in the Grail legend and have given a number of seminars on that topic.

I would like to introduce these comments by saying that I find his title and subtitle exceedingly appropriate, since, in a most provocative way, they call attention to the two major issues which confront readers of Chrétien de Troyes' *Perceval* and subsequent Grail stories. If Professor Fiedler can ask why the Grail Knight is Jewish and answer the question by means of a meditation concerning the Passover Seder, it is precisely because, and I hope you will pardon me the pun, this knight is indeed different from all other knights. We are in fact forced to ask ourselves why Perceval and Galahad seek something other than renown for death-dealing prowess or fidelity in an adulterous love and why the Grail ceremony is not merely the Holy Eucharist in its traditional form.

The question "why is the Grail Knight Jewish?" is rhetorically excellent, since it shocks us into realizing that we have forgotten an important aspect of the Grail legend. On the other hand it is slightly misleading; and I would like to rephrase it by asking: "Why is the Grail Knight Judeo-Christian?" If I am not mistaken, this is, ultimately, Professor Fiedler's main point. We are all too prone to think of this knight as Christian and forget the Jewish roots of his Christianity; but it would be equally wrong to stress only his Jewishness, which, in the case of Chrétien, cannot be demonstrated with absolute certainty. What should, I believe, be emphasized, is the way in which the spiritual torch is being passed from the Jew to the Christian. The Grail Knight, in subscribing to the New Law, is simultaneously transmitting the religious heritage of the Old Law to future generations. There is a definite rupture between the Old Law and the New, and this is often alluded to, but at the same time there is a very necessary spiritual continuity bridging the historical gap between the two.

Was this the meaning that Chrétien intended to convey through the mysterious happenings at the Fisher King's castle? Is the Grail procession Celtic, and therefore pagan, or should it be described as Christian or Jewish? Or could it possibly be a blend of the three? One thing seems obvious. The ceremony is intended to mystify the uninitiate. In other words it is ideally suited to the purpose of "making little boys ask questions." In my opinion no theory of origin proposed thus far fully accounts for all the noteworthy elements in the procession and in the meal served to Perceval and the Fisher King. In other words I am not in full agreement with a Celticist like Jean Marx or a Christian liturgist like Sister Amelia Klenke or with Professor Fiedler and my own student Eugene Weinraub, whose dissertation entitled "Chrétien's Grail: A Jewish Rite?" is soon to be published [see note 2 to Fiedler's article]. What seems important to me is that the scene portrayed by Chrétien is capable of evoking all three traditions and was perhaps created as a pedagogical device which would illustrate the necessity of a shift from the thinly veiled paganism of the chivalric code—the ceremonial hedonism mentioned by Professor Fiedler—to true Christianity firmly rooted in its Jewish past. If such is the case, then Chrétien may have planned to challenge the anti-Jewish statement made to Perceval by the penitent knight on Good Friday. One of his themes may in fact have been true charity. In other words "thou shalt not reject thy mother," if Perceval's mother does actually represent the Old Law, but at the same time "thou shalt not reject the New Law," which in a divinely ordained way continues the Old.

I fully sympathize with Professor Fiedler's statement that the Grail legend is a melancholy story. This is so, it seems to me, not only because the end of the Grail quest coincides with the end of the Arthurian world, but also because full communion between man and God, which I think is the ultimate goal of the quest, would put an end to all earthly delights. How many of us really desire paradise with the complete satiety it promises? Don't we in fact expect to be a trifle bored without the vanities of this world? I cannot help but think of the well-known passage in *Aucassin et Nicolette* in which Aucassin would rather be in hell with Nicolette, "his very sweet friend," than go to Heaven with all the pious of the earth. Lancelot and Guinevere and Paolo and Francesca somehow do strike us as more enjoyable companions than Galahad and Perceval's virgin sister. Since I am not certain that I have fully understood Professor Fiedler's line of reasoning, I eagerly await his reaction to my exegesis of his thesis.

STANLEY S. FERBER:

I would like to direct my remarks this morning at Professor Gutmann. It is traditional among Jews to say that every Jew must have two synagogues so that he can have one to which he doesn't go. In like manner there

must be at least two arguments so that one can be rejected. My friend and colleague Professor Gutmann has
been gracious enough to provide me with three arguments from which to choose. He has stated that Jewish
messianic conceptions were unique Jewish artistic expressions of diverse Judaisms in medieval Christian
Europe. This argument is, in my opinion, unassailable
and further presents us with a view of medieval Jewish
art which has long been needed. This is a synagogue to
which I can go with a very clear conscience.

Professor Gutmann's second argument is that Judaism made a considerable contribution to medieval Christian and Islamic art through its vast storehouse of biblical legends. This argument I adhere to less strongly
than the first. As I understand Dr. Gutmann's thrust, it
is not necessary to postulate a visual tradition among
the Jews in order to understand and explain the transmission and dispersal of specifically Jewish legends into
Christian and Muslim art. Literary sources of the Jewish legends, the Haggadot, are sufficient to explain the
transference. However I would like to raise a question
of how this Haggadic tradition from literary sources
finds its way into Christian art. Certainly the close relationship which existed between Muslims and Jews in
the East as well as the Jewish-Muslim relationship in
Spain would allow us to accept a close knowledge of
each other's literature, language, and legend, and the
commonality of sources in the mideast, predating the
rise of Muslim and early Christian times could also account for the entry of many of these Haggadic materials
into these cultures. Hence to find Jewish legend in Muslim art is an acceptable and expected phenomenon. But
again little has been done to explore this relationship,
and Dr. Gutmann's observations are welcome additions
to our body of knowledge.

My question, however, arises when we deal with
Christian art. Inasmuch as the knowledge of Hebrew
was not particularly widespread in medieval Europe
with the exceptions already mentioned, how would Jewish Haggadic material not found in the Church Fathers
find its way into medieval Christian art, especially when
knowledge tells us that much Haggadic and Midrashic
materials were used primarily to excoriate the Jews?
This doesn't preclude its use for other purposes, but
what the means of transmission may have been is one
question that indeed comes to mind. I would venture to
suggest that there may very well have been an illustrative tradition of Jewish origin available to the Christian
artists and that they were not solely dependent upon the
literary Haggadic sources. This conclusion is arrived at
in part at least, on the basis of the same visual material
Dr. Gutmann has shown us. The simplest illustration of
the Abram-Nimrod legend sequence from the Spanish
Haggadah is the one that shows Abraham leaning on a
staff before Nimrod without any other material illustrated. This appears in a Jewish manuscript and it assumes a knowledge of the legend on the part of the
viewer and thus need not illustrate it in all of its literal
aspects. The Christian illustrations of the legend, as
well as the Muslims', assumes no prior knowledge, or at
least not as great a degree of prior knowledge on the
part of the viewer, and hence illustrate either every step
of the story or epitomize the story in two or three key
sequences. We may surmise then that the Haggadah
illustration represents a tradition that existed either in-
dependently of, or minimally side-by-side with, the
textual traditions, but this particular point is certainly
open to more investigation. Thus although I may agree
with the formulation that Judaism made considerable
contributions to Christian and Islamic art, I would

hasten to add that we must carefully differentiate between the nature and quality of Jewish contributions to Christian and Muslim art and, second, be completely cognizant that this contribution need not have come solely from textual sources. This argument then is the synagogue into which I can go, but with the utmost caution.

Finally, my gracious disputant has supplied me with the third argument which I can both accept and reject. This is the statement that such controversies as the existence of early Jewish manuscript cycles or the permissibility of art among Jews are no longer a question. The only major recognition necessary is that there is a major discrepancy between what is preached by the rabbis and what is practiced by the people. Further it must be recognized that rabbinic opinion varied so that the hard iconoclastic line of the Hasmonean dynasty had already started to be softened by time of the Amoraim, the teachers of the second to the third centuries of the common era. This is the period of richest productivity of early Jewish art, and extant monuments include sculpture in the round, mosaic floors, both decorative and figural, fresco paintings on the walls of synagogues, Dura-Europos for example, and so on. From this point we proceed to really what is the thorniest question facing all students of Jewish and early Christian art—the existence of early Jewish manuscript cycles. Now I agree with Dr. Gutmann's conclusions that there is no substantiation available for the existence of early Jewish illustrative cycles. To point, however, to the Pamplona Bibles as the immediate source of the Spanish Haggadah illustration of the Egyptian princess standing nude in the waters with Moses and then state that the immediate source of the Pamplona Bibles has not yet been determined is really to beg the question. To say we need

not posit an early Jewish illustrative cycle to explain the
Spanish Haggadah tradition, but then say it can be explained by the Pamplona Bibles and say "however we
have not yet found the source of Pamplona Bibles," is
really not answering anything. Yet the greatest difficulty
facing scholars in this area is the necessity of an *argumentum ex silentio*. I would briefly like to propose a
possible avenue out of this dilemma and at the same
time offer myself for a *responsum* from Professor Gutmann.

One of the most perplexing manuscripts of the early
Christian period is the Ashburnham Pentateuch. It has
been variously dated from the fifth to the eighth centuries and has been given a provenance ranging from
North Africa to Spain or Provence or the North of Italy,
where it was supposedly executed by Syrian monks. All
of the above suggestions result from strange combina-
tions of the Latin text of Jerome's Vulgate translation
of the Bible and segments of the pre-Vulgate Itala
translation. In addition there is paleographic evidence
of the ninth-century work of the Tours school, the
Carolingian period, and painting as well as script suggestive of a French/Italian hand of a century earlier
perhaps. There is also a painting style which most closely resembles fifth- and sixth-century Coptic sources.
Obviously a manuscript of this sort presents us with
innumerable problems. I believe that a major obstacle
to unraveling the mystery of the Ashburnham Pentateuch has been that all scholars have unquestionably
considered it a Christian Bible. I would like to suggest
that we approach the Ashburnham Pentateuch as a late
surviving example of a class of illustrated Latin Bibles
produced for Jews in the Latin West. As such this class
of manuscripts would be analogous to the earliest Sep-
tuagints, that is, translations for those Jewish communi-

ties which had lost their ability to read Hebrew fluently, but which still practiced the religion of their fathers. I will attempt to demonstrate this hypothesis with two very brief examples from the manuscript's illustrative cycle, if you will bear with me.

The frontispiece on the manuscript is a depiction of an architectural shrine which has all the symbolic elements of a Torah shrine. There has been a good deal of scholarly controversy as to whether this is actually a Torah shrine or one of a very common class of late antique/early Christian architectural shrine motifs. Without taking the time to go into all of the arguments pro and con, I would support the contention that a Torah shrine is intended and further, following a suggestion made a number of years ago by Dr. Gutmann, that this particular moment represents a moment of unveiling the shrine to expose the Torah. Further we note the presence of the Hebrew names of the books of the Pentateuch transliterated in Latin. Jerome had used Latin transliterations of Hebrew words and the names of the books of the Pentateuch. So that use in itself is not inexplicable. However the concurrence of a motif which may very well be a Torah shrine with the transliterated Hebrew words is, minimally at least, suggestive. I would offer as an explanation of this suggestion my hypothesis that the Ashburnham Pentateuch was produced for a Latinized Jewish community in the West which had lost its ability to read Hebrew. There is ample evidence from Provence, the North of Spain, Narbonne, Troyes (Chrétien forgive us), that in this entire area Jewish communities existed that had lost their Hebrew and proceeded with their traditions in Latin. There are recorded cases where synagogues in Provence conducted services, sang psalms, in Latin. There is epigraphic evidence on tombstones with Latin inscriptions. Hence a Latin Bible for Jewish usage in this ambience is not at all unthinkable. But does this account for or in any way bear upon our problem of early Jewish biblical illustrative cycles? It would, if we could demonstrate that some part of the manuscript's illustrative cycle went back to an early source which was not prevalent or available at the time that the manuscript was produced. The illustration of Creation in this particular manuscript is, I believe, a case which can help us establish a very early date for an illustrative cycle. A number of years ago Bezalel Narkiss of the Hebrew University in Jerusalem discovered that there had originally been dual creative figures in the first four scenes of the Creation folio. Infra-red and X-ray photos revealed outlines of other figures. Again without going through all his arguments which I find convincing and extremely lengthy, however, let us say indeed there are dual Creation figures. They are very difficult to deny. Inasmuch as this manuscript has been associated with Spain in most of the early literature, Narkiss saw the Dual Creators as a reflection of the Adoptionist heresy prevalent in Spain during the seventh and eighth centuries. However the basic assumption that Narkiss made was that the manuscript was an original production of the seventh and eighth century in Spain and had no antecedents. All of the internal evidence of the manuscript suggests otherwise. A solution can be found if we assume the manuscript to be part of some Jewish tradition. I specifically emphasize "some Jewish tradition" because as Professor Gutmann himself has pointed out, there are many Judaisms with many faces. I would suggest that the Ashburnham Pentateuch reflects a Gnostic Jewish tradition going back to Egypt in the second century of the common era. Jewish Gnosticism believed in dual creators, and its belief was differentiated from prevalent Gnostic beliefs which also postulated a second creator—a demiurge accountable for, responsible for, those things which were not good, for the evil in the world, things which could not be assigned to the Supreme God, the positive creator. This was not so with Jewish Gnosticism. There is the figure Metatron, who is created in mystic Judaism, the second creator, the youthful young creator, the assistant to the one creator. In the Ashburnham Pentateuch there is no indication of separation of the two creators on the basis of good and evil or any other way. The only indication of separation is age. One creator is bearded and old, the other is somewhat younger.

Now in this brief time I cannot present fully all of the arguments in favor of this hypothesis. As a working assumption I would suggest that if it is true, it would provide the sorely missing evidence for a Jewish illustrative tradition in the earliest centuries of the Christian era. It would then be possible to include manuscript illumination with the numerous other arts practiced by the Jews in the second through the sixth centuries. So finally the *argumentum ex silentio* would be broken. Therefore I must graciously decline from entering the last of Dr. Gutmann's synagogues. Thank you.

REJOINDER:

PROFESSOR YOSEF YERUSHALMI:

In the time at my disposal I cannot possibly touch all bases. I tried to listen very carefully to what Mr. Cantor said, and I must confess that his critique leaves me baffled.

Mr. Cantor's charge is (a) that Jewish historians do

not use general categories, and (b) that they always claim the misery of the Jews is only the fault of the gentiles, while deliberately ignoring inner conflicts in Jewish society, and any trends that are not "rabbinic" or "nationalistic." I do not know what it was in my talk that gave him the impression that I share such a view of Jewish history. As for others, the very historians he says he wished me to discuss, Jewish historians all of them, are certainly innocent of the crimes he has listed. When Yitzhak Baer, for example, writes the history of the Jews of Spain, he devotes entire chapters to social and class conflicts within the Jewish community, and he has done so also in the many Hebrew monographs he has published.

The central issue raised by Mr. Cantor, however, really lies elsewhere, and it is somewhat more subtle. He does not, I take it, want us to talk about anything that smacks of a normative Judaism in the Middle Ages, because there were so many different "Judaisms." Well I don't know exactly what he means, though I quite understand his deeper motives for wanting to have it so. But by the same token there were many different kinds of Christianity as well in the Middle Ages, and there were all kinds of Christian heresies. I do not see that this fact has in any way inhibited historians who deal with the period up to the Reformation from assigning a dominant place to the Catholic Church in the religious history of medieval Europe, and I do not see that the Talmudic-rabbinic tradition should be treated any differently in this respect. As for "nationalist" Judaism, the fact remains that prior to the modern era the Jews perceived themselves, and were considered by gentiles, as a nation in exile united by a hope of ultimate restoration to Zion. Mr. Cantor may not approve of this, but the

historical record on this score is both abundant and un-
ambiguous.

I am drawing to a close; I told you I could not touch
all bases. I will tell Mr. Cantor and all of you, ladies
and gentlemen, that I began to formulate my address
long before I even saw the program (that you may take
on faith). When I saw the actual program, in its very
structure I found confirmation of what I intended to
say. Now, having heard the actual papers, I must tell
you that except perhaps for a phrase here and there, I
find nothing to change or to retract, and I will tell you
exactly what I mean.

I called my address "Jewish History from Within and
from Without." What I am about to say has nothing
to do with the substantive merits or the stimulating
qualities of any individual paper we have heard. But we
were talking about "Jewish history from within and
from without." I came to this conference, and what I
have heard in a symposium on—mind you—"*Jewish
Culture* in the Middle Ages" was one paper that really
had to do with medieval Jewish culture, and that was
the paper of Mr. Stillman. Otherwise I heard from
Rosemary Ruether what allegedly (because I share some
of the strictures voiced from [SMU]) was the attitude
of the Church Fathers toward the Jews. I do not think
that is "Jewish culture." You may as well go to a symposium on American culture and listen to a paper on what
the French think of the Americans. I heard a paper on
anti-feminism and antisemitism in the medieval *Spanish*
literary tradition which I would love to hear at a meeting of Hispanists but not in one devoted to medieval
Jewish culture. Here, if anything, we should have been
informed on the antifeminine and profeminine tradition
in Spanish Hebrew poetry. We should have heard about

Judah Ibn Shabbetai's poem *Sonh ha-nashim* ("The Women-Hater"), a twelfth-century work that was answered in the thirteenth-century by a poet named Isaac, who wrote *Ezrat nashim* ("Help to the Women"). Again, I heard an interesting paper on art that I can't quite put into a slot on either side, but I think the bulk of it had to do with what the Jews (unwittingly) provided as themes for *Christian art*, rather than a substantive discussion of some aspect of Jewish art in the Middle Ages. And then I was led seductively into the enchanted forest of Mr. Fiedler's imagination, and I was offered a problem that is fascinating in itself, namely, "Why is the Grail Knight Jewish?"; but I assure you that this was never a problem for the Jews of Troyes. In short, you learned much from every paper at this symposium. But how much did you really learn about "Jewish Culture in the Middle Ages"?

PROFESSOR NORMAN STILLMAN:

I must say I find it rather difficult to respond to any direct way, since I don't find any direct critique that I can really answer. The only thing I would like to point out is that I agree with Mr. Cantor's very good point on the problem of the class difference in medieval Jewry which is something to which we haven't addressed ourselves properly until now. Recently my own teacher and master Shelomo Dov Goitein gave a very penetrating talk entitled "Basic Problems in Jewish History" at the World Congress of Jewish Studies in Jerusalem, in which he points to this continual element in Jewish society going all the way back to Talmudic times of the merchant scholar. We have many of the Talmudic rabbis, who, we are told, dealt in Metaxa or in the silk trade, so this seems to be something that is true. I agree with Mr. Cantor's assessment to some extent as far as Spain is concerned and perhaps as far as Europe is concerned, although there I am purely speaking as a dilettante. For the Middle East, though, it is not so clear. I think the oppression of the masses is a bit of an exaggeration. I don't think the Jewish masses in the Middle East were such downtrodden individuals, although there certainly were very sharp distinctions between the upper, lower, and middle classes. The Geniza letters are filled with references to petty merchants and shopkeepers, using such terms as "beggars," "these people," etc., and of course we have large welfare roles from Fustat. Good people from better families are referred to as "sons of people" or other such titles. We do know that the upper middle class did very much assimilate into the mores of their society. The use of concubine slave girls, although concubinage is legal in Judaism, the using of your slave girl, for example, for sexual purposes is very strictly forbidden, although we have many cases where this was ignored. There were tensions, but it is very difficult of course to talk about *Klassenkampf* when you are speaking about this period because we don't have very much information beyond the middle-middle class. The Geniza, as a matter of fact, reflects mostly middle-middle-class merchants. We don't have that much material, even on the upper classes. Most of the sectarian movements that break out seem to have socioeconomic as well as theological backgrounds. Naturally when you are dealing with a theocratic society, the only way you can express any form of opposition is theologically, and one of the little-known outbreaks of a Jewish rebellion which is in Korasan and Transoxania seems to come from people of the working class. There is Abu Isa al-Isfahani's rebellion in the seventh century; according to the Muslim and Jewish writers that tell us about him, he was a tailor. The whole beginning of Karaism seems to go back to "working class" (I don't like to use the term "working class," of course, when you are talking about this period, but it goes back to a lower stratum of society in the East).

If I am permitted, could I just make two comments perhaps on the other papers, if that is at all permissible. One on Professor Ferber's thesis on the Latin Bible for Jews: I think that that is a very good point, although we don't have any Latin Bibles for Jews. We have the Bible almost in every other vernacular that they spoke. My only question on that point is that in almost every example (with the exception of course of the Septuagint during the Hellenistic period) when Jews use their local vernacular for liturgy or Scripture, they always use the Hebrew script. Every example we have, be it Judaeo-Provencal/Judaeo-Persian. We do have Judaeo-Latin, we have poems in Latin in Hebrew script and even people who could not read Hebrew script—sorry, the Bible in its original Hebrew, the first thing that anyone did learn was the Hebrew script. So I would be very hesitant before I would accept that point.

The other point is on the business of the Gnostic tradition in the West, specifically Gnostic or Dualist Jewish tradition. Again maybe I come from the cowardly school of history, but I am afraid that unless I have more evidence, I am very hesitant on that one also. Our only strong information as far as Jewish Dualists and Gnostics are concerned comes from the further east of the Islamic world, especially from Transoxania and Khorasan, which by the way, was one of the early homes of Karaism. We see, for example, Saadia, who fights against this so strongly, but we don't seem to find that as a problem further west. It's not mentioned in the

Jewish sources as a problem at any rate. That would be my only other comment.

PROFESSOR GOLDBERG:

I would like to respond to Professor Adams's suggestion about the use of the word "patristic." It seems to me that in the Hispanic tradition, at any rate, people who were writing antifeminist materials called upon patristic sources for their information. Professor Adams mentioned Augustine. I think offhand of his talking about the fact that the knowledge of the angels was not transmitted to the Jews because they are a carnal people and they speak to God only in a carnal way asking for good crops and success in life and that this was Augustine (it isn't a very vituperative reference to Jews, but it was his attitude toward Jews). Augustine also pointed out that women lost the vote, citing that old story about Minerva (Athena really, I should say) and the naming of Athens, when one woman's vote swung the decision so that Athens was Athens and was not named after Poseidon. The God of the Sea got pretty cross and as a result cooked up a storm, if you remember, and did in fact punish the city so that from then on women were no longer allowed to vote, nor were they any longer allowed to transmit their names to their children. These were the two punishments of the God of the Sea. Well, Augustine tells this story and it seems to me pretty clear that even in such a reasonable Church Father as Augustine we find these references and I'm not even talking about the other more vituperative ones. The other part of it is that the exemplary tradition is a clear indication that women and Jews were the enemies of the Church. All of the *exempla* were used—Maria Rosa Lida de

Malkiel, a Hispanist, certainly suggests it and I think so does Jean-Thomas Welter (you will forgive me if I am not pronouncing his name properly) suggest that the *exempla* were used primarily to enliven sermons obviously, and in the *exempla* tradition you all know what kind of vituperative material there is against women.

I would also like to suggest the least common denominator to which Professor Adams refers is the institution of matrimony; both women and Jews did indeed in a rather direct way threaten the sexual mores and the structure of matrimony in the society with which I was dealing and I admit it was a very limited society. I would also like to comment just very briefly on that reference to the story about Chrysostom, which turns up not in a collection of Jewish *exempla* but in a collection of Christian *exempla* collected by Clemente Sánchez Vercial, published in the fifteenth century, but really is a kind of ABC of *exempla* from the whole Hispanic tradition.

I would also just briefly like to refer to what Professor Yerushalmi said, "Jews in the Middle Ages cannot have existed in a vacuum." They must indeed have been touched or have been aware of the pressures from the outside society, so that I think that even here in a study of Jewish culture, one must recognize that Jewish culture existed outside of, next to perhaps, but in conjunction with even the Hispanic culture. Thank you.

PROFESSOR GUTMANN:

I only wish I could very strongly disagree with Professor Ferber, but I am much more inclined to enter his synagogue than he is aware of. As a matter of fact I would be the first to rejoice if indeed an illustrated He-

brew or a Jewish manuscript could be found in some
Near Eastern cave or dig to finally solve the problem
not only of the origins of Christian art, but of the missing links of the Dura-Europos synagogue paintings as
well as of the later illuminated Hebrew manuscript
traditions. The strongest evidence for the existence of
ancient illuminated Jewish manuscripts is the Ashburnham Pentateuch. In my younger days, with the enthusi-
asm of youth, when I was working with Professor
Charles Rufus Morey, I wrote a thesis on the Ashburnham Pentateuch and claimed that its model was a Jewish manuscript and is indeed the missing link. But, you
know, as one gets older, one grows more conservative
and cautious, and I am no longer as certain of my earlier
hypothesis as I was in those days. I still believe that the
old question of illustrated manuscripts among Jews, as
far as the evidence is concerned today, is an argument
from silence and very highly problematical. I am willing to leave the question open, hoping that one of these
days something will be discovered to finally settle this
interesting, but difficult argument.

Let me add two footnotes to what Dr. Ferber has
said. First, Professor Narkiss of the Hebrew University,
with whom I spoke last summer, does believe that the
Ashburnham Pentateuch has antecedents and that it
ultimately goes back to the Near East, possibly to models found in Syria. As a matter of fact he is convinced
that there are two models behind the Ashburnham Pentateuch and he's now preparing a major study on this
manuscript. In support of your theory, Professor Ferber,
one can note that the division of the Bible into five
books, the Pentateuch, is a typically semitic way of dividing the Bible. In the West we don't find that too often;
usually it's the Octateuch, the Heptateuch, etc., but not
the Pentateuch. In addition, another very strong argu-

ment as far as the Ashburnham Pentateuch is concerned
is the inclusion of many haggadic traditions in its
miniatures that seem to go back to the *targumic* or the
midrashic literature. So, far from disagreeing with you,
I am almost over in your camp, except that I am more
skeptical—perhaps because I'm a little older than you.
When you get to my hoary age, you too will approach
this issue with a little more caution. At the present time
I leave the whole question open, since I don't think the
evidence presented is that strong to support your position.

PROFESSOR FIEDLER:

Chiefly what I want to say to you is thank you. I feel as
if I have been a guest here invited into your house,
which didn't seem to me an unfamiliar house, but on
the other hand is not one I visit very frequently. I apolo-
gize if I misled anybody into thinking in advance that
I was going to talk about Jewish culture in the Middle
Ages from the inside. To do that would be to peddle
books before the door of Confucius. I wouldn't offend
you by doing so, but I thought it might be interesting to
you if we could meet. I mean if I could take you out of
your own context into my—I call it my "Enchanted
Forest"—and if we could converse there a little while.
The comments on my talk have really heartened me because they indicate to me that a conversation has really
gone on, that communication has truly happened, which
seems to me in scholarly circles more extraordinary than
it ought to be. I was listened to, I was responded to by
a temperament which I feel is very different from my
own, but somehow we were in touch for a moment as
we went on our various ways—"I go to Hell with Ni-

colette and who has chosen the better way? Only the God knows."

I did want to emphasize, since I have the last chance to talk, two points in my remarks, namely, the kind of two margins or parameters of my remarks which were not summarized and which begin to seem more and more important to me. Though I am by no means an expert in Jewish culture of the Middle Ages, I did want to set the beginning of the Grail story in a context of Jewish culture and to talk about the school of Rashi and Troyes and to talk about the particular moment in the relationship of the Jews and the Christians in Europe at which Chrétien was writing his poem, a moment when Jewish refugees were coming into the city of Troyes to escape from persecution. You know, I live in a funny world; I want to be at the same time in the Enchanted Forest and yet to root it in history someplace.

The other thing that intrigues me is that though I had not intended it when I began writing it, by the time I came to the end of my remarks, it had become clear to me that it is impossible to talk about the view of Jews in the Christian mind of Europe in the twelfth century, let's say, without also talking about women. The two things truly come together. I suddenly realize that behind my title and in the back of my head, as I did not realize at first, there was an absolutely ridiculous but somehow provocative talk, which I heard many years ago which was called "Was the Wife of Bath Jewish?". The point of that talk, of course, was that Jews and women were used from time to time by different people and in varying ways throughout the Middle Ages to project a certain kind of hostility to something profoundly alien and in some sense unassimilable into the major tradition. It is interesting to me that in the Grail story the problem of persecution of Jews is made much harder for the imagination of gentile Christian, Christian gentile, however one says, because the Jews are represented not as a grim father who is easy to dismiss, not as the High Priest, let's say, but represented as the mother. The figure of the mother of the Grail knight of Perceval surely fades into the figure of Mary, the mother of Jesus as the Messiah, and when the Jews are thought of in maternal terms, then the problem of the casting off of the Jews becomes very intense. It seems to me it leads directly to the good word which the hermit gives, though it comes out of a very different mouth. I don't think that Chrétien would have ended up by in any way opposing the antisemitic remarks, but I think what he was willing to do, having an immensely complicated mind, was to put on record his own deep ambivalence on the subject which must have been the ambivalence of the culture in which he lived.

AFTERWORDS

FATHER SYNAN:

Before these "afterwords" there were, of course, the words that the reader has just read. Cold print can hardly convey the music to which many of the words that made up our *disputatio* were pronounced. We can do no more than assure the reader that text and melody were consonant: the passion at which the written transcript hints was unmistakable. Professor François Bucher, codirector of the Center, had expressed beforehand his hope that "blood would flow"; in the real, if rhetorical, sense that he intended, blood flowed indeed. Thanks to disagreements, some expressed with passion,

all with candor, our *disputatio* could not have been ar-
raigned for a defect of credibility; dissent was real and
was seen to have been real. Our Sunday morning "jousting of the clerks" may not have qualified as high tragedy, but we may hope it proved to be as cathartic for
disputants and for their audience as Aristotle thought
tragedy ought to be (*Poetics* 6; 1449 b 20–32).

Still, what we regretted most was less the violence of
some of the jousting than the absence of one key duel-
list. As all conference organizers are taught by experience, the very eminence that prompts them to choose
participants entails a risk of truncated attendance. Precisely because they are eminent, those participants are
in demand and bilocation is beyond them. By a particularly unfortunate happenstance, the calm and judicious
critique by Professor Jeremy duQ. Adams was delivered
in the absence of Professor Rosemary Ruether; it was
intriguing, but frustrating, to wonder how she might
have met his challenge.

Not everything, however, was excessively solemn in
our deliberations at that concluding session. How often
does a learned conference hear so apposite a pun as the
question put by Professor Alice Colby concerning the
Grail Knight as Professor Leslie Fiedler had presented
him? "Why is this Knight different from all other
knights?"

Nor was the polemic side (the inevitable emphasis
of a *disputatio*) the most significant aspect of the conference as a whole. Without a doubt what came through
as the most striking disclosure of all was the variety
and wealth of medieval Jewish life as the scholars of
our day are recovering it. In every direction in which
the conference probed, simplistic estimates were shown
to be bankrupt. Like the Jewish reality of our own time,
that of the Middle Ages broke through all stereotypes.

A bewildering complexity of medieval Jewish cultural achievements provoked an astonishing multiplicity of gentile response. Seen "from within," or seen "from without," to borrow the rubrics under which Professor Yerushalmi made his contribution, restricted to the Jewish presence in Islamic Spain with Professor Norman Stillman, or to Spanish literary tradition with Professor Harriet Goldberg, the Jewish fact was obviously richer than can be trapped in any single "image"—Professor Joseph Gutmann could speak of an "image" only with the expansions: "conceptions," "contributions," "controversies."

On Sunday morning Professor Stanley Ferber had the penultimate word, Professor Norman Cantor a word of dissent, and my word was the last word, naturally one of thanks to SUNY-Binghamton. Here it is our hope to give all those words a measure of permanence and in the traditional way, for it was no mistake to call us, Jews and Christians, "People of the Book," and so we have made this small book from the words that filled those days of conference.

This controversial book offers a detailed, chronological, reading of all Milton's major works including a chapter devoted to his prose. Furthermore, it is the first substantial effort in English literary criticism to employ the theories of the Structuralist school with a particular emphasis on the methods of such figures as Barthes, Girard and Foucault. As a comprehensive reading of Milton and in light of its methodological aim, this book should attract a wide readership within both literary and cultural studies.

Professor Bouchard explores Milton's development as a poet and his increasing sensitivity to the 'contamination' implicit in the act of writing – a theme generally argued by Milton scholars in terms of the Satanic impulse underlying the construction of *Paradise Lost*. The present interpretation supports this argument, but it shows, as well, that *Paradise Lost* is Milton's resolution of the paradox (of the devout, yet supposedly blasphemous poet) through an art which is fundamentally iconoclastic. In this sense, the poem creates a new reflexive and reflective art in opposition to the Renaissance stress on mimesis.